FROM CLEATS
TO LOAFERS

Keep working hard!

FROM CLEATS TO LOAFERS

AND EVERYTHING IN BETWEEN

JARED A. JOHNSTON

CONTENTS

"Faith is seeing light with your heart, when all your eyes see is darkness"

-Barbara Johnson

"This is your testing time. You have been reduced to poverty and humiliated in order that you might be forced to discover your "other self.""

-Napoleon Hill

PREFACE

Early morning workouts were a staple for allowing me to come across certain achievements in my athletic career. From a Schumann underclassmen quarterback MVP, being blessed to play in a high school all-star game for my state's region, to receiving a football scholarship at my junior colleges and my four-year university, being able to start on the college level and break a few records; early morning workouts were always a part of my routine. But this early morning moment was something that I had never once experienced. It was different-very different. It was about three-thirty in the morning. A year earlier, at this time, I would more than likely have been waking up to go to the gym or head to the field to work on my game.

On this particular morning, however, there was no music playing through my headphones to get me ready for the workout. It was just myself and my thoughts. These thoughts were not the usual ones of me visualizing my success for the upcoming season I was going to embark on; a season that I believed would get me started in the right direction, to move up the professional ranks. Those thoughts that I was accustomed to would give me an extra push on early mornings when my body didn't quite want to get out of the bed. This particular morning though the thoughts that consumed me were not positive but were instead ones of helplessness coupled with the feelings of being valueless, worthless, uncertain, unfulfilled, and unsuccessful. I wasn't heading for my workout. No, that morning, with these thoughts invading my head I found myself sitting on the couch, shoulders hunched, head sunk, tears flowing, and a sharp Knife in my hand. How could I even get to this point in life to think of harming myself? This for sure was not me.

The answer is simple, I was faced with the harsh realization that my dream of being a professional athlete would not come to fruition. My career in football was being cut prematurely. I am not the only one who has faced this situation. It can be one of the toughest moments in a football player's life, regardless of their age, gender, ethnic background or socioeconomic status. Personally, as a twenty-three-year-old, that moment came with tremendous heartbreak and confusion. Suddenly it was time for my life to take on a new beginning-one that was unplanned and for which I was unprepared. I had ended my journey and quickly began to notice how the pursuit of the NFL can impact young men in a negative way. This is especially true if players do not prepare themselves effectively or have a support system of families, friends, coaches, and schools that they are blessed with. This in turn can leave them lost when it comes time for them to make a post-athletic transition.

For those that do make it and are able to enjoy a prosperous and healthy career, the NFL is the ultimate blessing. It provides these athletes the opportunity to make money doing something they love as a professional career, allows them the chance to become financially secure, enables them to pay their parents back for all of their hard work and-from that point forward-gives them the ability to change the trajectory of their family and build a legacy.

It makes me think-what does the NFL dream become for an athlete who expended themselves to perfect their craft, possessed the talent, willpower, mindset and faith to play on the NFL level, but fell short?

For the tens of thousands of those who had dreams and aspirations of playing football as a career professionally, there are tens of thousands of young men annually heading into the "real world" with sudden depression, feelings of embarrassment, failure, a lack of self-worth, and a loss of identity as they fail to realize their life-long dream. I am sure that there are several who move on from the sport just as smooth as ever; however, this book is geared towards those who come upon struggles once they are no longer a part of the sport, they were so passionate about.

These athletes are left with the feeling of having to start all over, and transitioning into the next phase of life can be a very daunting task. Although daunting, know at the end of the tunnel there is more than enough room for success.

CHAPTER ONE

DREAM DEFERRED

From the smell of the grass to the butterflies before each game to the feeling of strapping up the shoulder pads to lacing up the cleats and the locker room shenanigans, what I wouldn't give to be back in meetings or rushing to the cafeteria to eat dinner after practice or hurrying to get to team chapel on time. From the everyday grind of the game, the early morning workouts at 5am when I was still half asleep, the lengthy film sessions, the numerous number of sprints in the middle of the summer, and the long practices for two-a-day's that I hated, I loved being a part of it all. From the joy of seeing your work from the week pay off on game day and all the smiles and laughter after a last second touchdown to win a game to the tears and pain felt after a loss realizing that any chance at a conference championship was now in the past-, I cherish those memories. The will you are forced to find deep within yourself to push through that last set in the weight room, the security you felt walking onto any field knowing your brothers have your back and you have got theirs in return, the long bus drives for away games laughing with my teammates and coaches with no care in the world-all these imprinted themselves on my life. Football brought me an indescribable amount of happiness. But it also brought a tremendous amount of pain, when I realized it was time to let the game-and my time in it-go.

You see with football there was always something to look forward to, always something to set my sights on-no matter what was going on in my personal life. For 16 years, I always knew I would be right back at it. But now there were no winter workouts, no summer workouts, no spring ball to look forward to. I realized that I would never have any of those experiences again as a player. Reality hit me, and to be honest, it made me think that I made the wrong decision. I began to believe that all the years of hard work had been for nothing. What do you do as an athlete who has sacrificed years of their life for one sole purpose, just to get to a point in your life where you realize that you have failed? After investing an ample amount of time into the sport, at the end of it all there was no return on my investment, no outcome I had worked so hard to achieve.

Like me, you will find yourself in a state of confusion, facing possibly one of the hardest decisions in your life: taking another route and having to figure out if you are giving up or moving on. How can you live your life believing the saying "you can do anything you want to do in this world?" You may begin to question if that saying is even true. At this point, you have done everything in your power and may have had the skill set to match, however, you are not doing the one thing you sacrificed your whole life to do. You may have written down your goals, visualized your success-a method that is supposed to lead you to the end goal-, and put in an extreme amount of hard work and faith, yet you have seen none of your vision come into fruition. You will look at others who have gained the position that you were sure you would be in and wonder to yourself "why?" or "how come this guy made it but I did not?" You may have worked harder than the individual and may even have been more talented. You will reflect on the past years and wonder if you personally should have done something different: perhaps performing better in high school academically in order to attend a bigger school, which would enhance your chances at making it to the NFL.

A lot of us believed that our purpose was to play football, take care of our families, and maybe have a platform to lift others up and be a light to millions of people-a display of hope and positivity. However, when we reach the point where we realize that it will not work out, we must decide to find the good in the bad and the success in the failure. Maybe football was your purpose, for that season of your life; now it is time to transition into the next stage, which will bring on a much greater purpose if you allow it. It's this "if" that many of us struggle with immediately after our dreams fall through.

Throughout this book you will learn about one of the most vital areas in an athlete's life-the area that if treated and grown properly can enhance your life or if gone about the wrong way can lead you down a dark path. This area is the transition phase.

It can test your mental makeup, as well as your faith and the relationships that you have built throughout your life. This book will provide you with a blueprint on how to transition through life after your playing days are over, as well as offer insight on how to plan so you are better equipped when that moment comes. I will share with you my personal experiences, my internal thoughts and struggles, and stories of athletes around me who have played on every professional level and who I have had the opportunity to observe both from close relationships and from a distance. All of these helped me generate this blueprint in order to help as many athletes as I can and bring them to understand they are not alone in this transition phase.

Now whether your highest level of playing was college, AFL, CFL, or the NFL, or you are reading this book while currently playing on the college or professional level and still pursuing your dream ask yourself these questions: Am I more than prepared to move on successfully when it is time to hang it up, especially if it is not on my terms? Am I prepared to accept my life when the dream I have worked for now becomes a dream deferred? When my time came, I believed the answer was yes, of course I am. However, I was sorely mistaken.

What happens to a dream deferred?
Does it dry up
like a raisin in the sun?
Or fester like a sore—
And then run?

Does it stink like rotten meat?
Or crust and sugar over—
like a syrupy sweet?

Maybe it just sags
like a heavy load.

Or does it explode?

If you are or were a casual athlete, just playing the sport because it is fun or because your parents wanted to allow you some leisure time, you may not be able to relate- and quite frankly this book is not for you. This book is geared towards the athlete who believed football was their only option. Those who ate, drank, and slept football every single day, believing that their dream would become a reality no matter how hard it seemed. The ones that ultimately failed to reach their goal, as well as those who may begin to doubt or fear that they will come up against struggles once they leave the sport. Those of you who may have come to a point in your life where you feel like you have maxed out all that you have to offer the world. You may be in a place of sadness, discomfort, confusion, bitterness, or depression, you may even begin to have suicidal thoughts-, and all these feelings may last for a week, a few months or even years. This book will prove that you are far from alone in how you feel. Many others have experienced the same exact pain and heartbreak; therefore, you should not be ashamed.

My intention is to talk about the truth and topics nobody wants to discuss; nobody ever talks about the downside too much. Now, I am not here to be a dream killer; I am not here to tell anyone that they cannot make football their career. I say work your tail off and pursue your goals, but along the way make it a priority to begin to intentionally set yourself up for future success off the playing field. Coincidently, along this journey you may find your purpose, so be aware and enjoy the beauty of this process. We know everyone will not make it to the NFL, if an individual is blessed to it is not guaranteed that they will be successful in the league. But the thing I love is seeing the faith in athletes when they work tirelessly for years, believing wholeheartedly that they will be the one to make it. The major issue is that when we realize we are not "the one," we tend to lose the faith and confidence we once possessed in our ability to take on the world. It is important to make sure that the faith you display is transferrable to every area of your life. My goal is to help those in need who are going through a similar situation that I found myself in and lend a helping hand to those who may began to doubt themselves as their playing days dwindle and come to an end. If anything at all, I would like for you to just think and do some self-reflection. This story is about realizing that we all come to a point in our lives where the one thing we loved is no longer a part of our daily lives: when we need to find our true selves, when we need to make a decision that will shape the trajectory of our lives and our future generations.

Tell it like it is

. . .

Coaches, mentors, however you want to describe them, often tell players the stats on who is going to make it and who is not. They talk about the importance of having a "back-up plan" and making good grades. They do not tell you that when you are in college and 110% dedicated to your respective program, you do not have time for a "back-up plan" most of the time. They make it seem as though it will be a very natural and easy transition; they do not mention falling into depression and dealing with extreme frustration They do not tell you how it can be a very hard hump to get over. Let's face it, after ten, fifteen, and in some cases, twenty plus years of immersing oneself into one dream, one goal, you come up short, and it is not the easiest thing to effortlessly move past. Most times the athlete is left to discover their new life all on their own. They do not tell the overly focused and dedicated athlete that they will need to find themselves again, once they are finished. I hope that you find at least the smallest ounce of advice, help, or direction to benefit you. My time of sadness, depression and overall feeling of "what in the world am I supposed to do now!!??", I hope will benefit you. They say the best teacher is experience, I disagree. The best teacher is another person's mistakes; therefore, take note of my mistakes and learn from them, so you in turn will have the upper hand when you find yourself in a similar situation.

CHAPTER TWO

WHAT HAPPENED TO HIM??

We often hear the glory stories of 5-star athletes that go on to play at a top college: then go on to play professionally for 10+ years and have a successful career. Or the under the radar player who does not get noticed until they reach the professional level and become an "overnight sensation," which the world perceives but was the result of relentless years of hard work. However, very rarely do we hear about the "rejects," the "almost made it" group of athletes. For instance, what about the top all American that does make it to the NFL then cannot make it past training camp? Or the top pick who is out of the league within 1-2 years, leaving them to become just an afterthought, if even a thought at all? Or the player from the small school who knows that he can play with the D-I athletes and is more than capable of playing at the highest level, who finally gets his chance as an undrafted free agent and never sees an NFL field after rookie minicamp? Or the athlete who has professional scouts come to numerous practices, but on draft day his name is not called and never receives an invite to camp? What about the guy who takes the route of semi-pro, AFL, or CFL, then finally reaches their lifelong dream of the NFL and 6 months to a year later they're cut and never make it back to the big leagues? Or the guy who never even makes it past the lower levels of the professional leagues but has undeniable talent? Or the 5-star athlete in high school who is dubbed as the next great thing on the front page of magazines and talked up as a sure fire NFL draft pick, but once they hit college they struggle to see the field and you never hear of them again? After all the praise and accolades what does the athlete have to show for it, if they are not playing at the highest level and not achieving their goal? What happens? Do they just accept it with a huge smile on their face and walk off into a story book ending? Do they walk into a corporate office and immediately learn to love what they are doing? Do they wake up every day with the goal driven purpose they had when they were pursuing their dream? Do they even feel they have a purpose anymore? Do they finish college and walk across the stage and receive their degree? Or do they fall into a depressed state of mind and fail to even finish school? Do they feel their life has come to an end figuratively speaking? Or is this the beginning of their life? Is it really that easy to move on and transition from a sport you believed you could do forever?

In 2016 an article posted by "The Oregonian" included a piece from the mother of one of the better corners to come out of Oregon and one of the top collegiate football players in his class, Cliff Harris. His play on the field proved he was worthy of being a top NFL draft pick. However, he was not drafted. Issues off the field in college caused him to be kicked off the Oregon football team and resulted in him becoming an undrafted free agent. Once Harris got his shot in the league, he was unable to solidify an NFL position, and he spent his time bouncing from team to team. The deviant behavior that caused issues in college continued once he was released from the NFL. After a mugshot of the athlete was released his mother took to Facebook to share her thoughts and respond to individuals who took pleasure in her son's trials and tribulations post football. She stated, "To see your child go from a happy, outgoing and confident person into a hurting and painful person is a very hurtful thing to see. He always wished he could give me the world and wanted to give back to his community for he knew where he came from. I watched my son go from an all-out football great with many friends and followers, to not one call or a hello from you." She went on to say, "Regardless of Cliff going through one of the hardest times of his life, regardless of him fighting through all of the demons that are trying to destroy him and regardless of him never becoming that NFL LOCKDOWN CORNER. He will always be my son. I am going to always love him and be there for him." Reading that, and knowing it came from a mother, who is most often the closest person to a young male touched home and resonated with me: I mean who knows their son better than a mother? This situation and the expression of truth from a mother barely scratches the surface of some of the issues we may face when we are detached from the sport for good.

Latwan Anderson, one of the top athletes in the country coming out of high school in the 2010 class and ranked as the number one player in his state-with dreams of playing at USC-, seemed to be on the path to a prosperous college and NFL career. His high school team was filled with future soon-to-be NFL talent, but out of all the talent he was projected to be the best. Unfortunately, his dreams of college and NFL success never came to fruition. What did come to fruition is a seven-year jail sentence.

After discovering that his dream school, USC, was geographically too far away for his family's liking, Anderson chose a different path. He stated, "I just thought about playing football at USC and once I couldn't do that my dream was crushed, so I made up my mind to go somewhere warm and have fun." That warm place was in South Florida, at the University of Miami. This is where he became too involved in the party life of Miami and was eventually removed from the university. He attended several junior colleges with no positive results, leading him to return to his hometown of Cleveland, Ohio. After not hearing about or seeing one of the top recruits coming out of high school in 2010 playing on Saturdays, several may have wondered what happened to him?

In his words: "I pretty much lost control. It's hard to be a kid and have all that attention-have everybody love you today and hate you tomorrow." The problem itself is deeper than a one-month span of very bad decisions. What happened to him happened long before he was arrested and sentenced to prison. Sometimes "what happened" to the athlete is not necessarily a set of events that happen once they finish playing. Parents, coaches, and friends need to be aware of situations that negatively affect the athlete, situations which come back to deter the athlete after they are finished playing. Some may claim that the reason former athletes act out is because they are done with football; this is not true in all situations. These issues may have been there all along; however, society focuses on the performance of the player and fails to dig deep into the athlete's life. Take away football and the issues rise to the surface. Anderson's high school coach, who was known to take inner-city kids and help create many success stories, stated that Anderson never had a solid foundation to begin with. His head coach did his best to improve Anderson's life, but he said that the year he had with him simply was just not enough time. Another problem was that Anderson displayed a lack of trust in people. To everyone else around Anderson, football was priority, and Anderson, the individual, was second. Anderson stated "Yea, I have the spotlight, but at the end of the day, who really cares about who I am, or do you really just care that I can score touchdowns?" As his career ended, Anderson had growing pressure, especially considering he now had a daughter to care for. Growing up in an environment where football was deemed the only possible way to escape from whichever trappings him or his family may have dealt with and possessing no other knowledge or skills developed outside of football, he became more and more desperate for money. This culminated in three robberies within a month in 2016. The final was brutally violent, in which a loaded gun was held to the head of a gas station clerk. Ultimately, these acts sent him to prison for 7 years.

When people ask what happened to a forgotten star, there are many stories about an athlete who is suddenly stuck and lost after they finish playing. I could fill several more pages with these stories. If you look up the top 100 players of any class from former years you will find that rarely do they achieve a long NFL career, and this is only focusing on the top 100. It does not account for the thousands more who face a similar reality. For those that move right into a career or job, there are several more who are left lost and consumed with feelings of dejection. Many say that all they focused on was football, and that is all they cared about. How does it affect a young person's mind after being praised and worshipped throughout their life only to face reality and end up back home at square one with numerous questions running through their mind?

CHAPTER THREE

WHO, WHAT, WHEN & WHY?

W hat am I going to do now? Will I be happy? Is this what I really want to do? Will I get bored within two years? How am I going to provide for my family? Should I have chosen to play a different sport? Should I have picked a different major? Are all my dream's dead? Are all my goals now pushed under the rug?

There is a plethora of questions that race through a football player's mind once they are done with the sport.

One of the most daunting questions, I believe, is when we question if we will still be successful. Seeing that football may have been the only avenue some of us felt would allow us to reach a level of high success, this is a valid question. I believe that success has a very broad meaning; to me, it is such a general statement. It must be defined. What is success to you? Is it being a millionaire? Is it being the first in your family to graduate college? Is it buying your dream car or is it having a 7-bedroom house with a back yard for your children to enjoy? Is it being able to give back, get out of the hood, travel and explore the world, have a stable 9-5 job or make it to the NFL? You see what I mean? Success can be displayed in so many fashions.

Before you arrive at what will feel like a dead end- the end of your playing days that is-you should define what success means to you personally or at least be able to form a vision of what it would look like.

Know that at the end of the day football or a million-dollar contract is not the determining factor for who you are as a person. Success for myself was making it to the NFL, doing something I absolutely love, having a great career, and signing a coveted multi-million-dollar contract. All this I felt would grant me the opportunity to take care of my family: making sure my parents did not have to work, setting them up for retirement, putting my whole family on one block so I know everyone is well and taken care of, traveling the world, being able to give back and help those in need. I also wanted to have such a great impact on the world that I could change it. People always harp on money not being that important; any person who says that has lost their mind and is a fool. I knew exactly what I wanted to do with the money and how it would be used for positive outreach. I didn't want it to go splurge and stunt on a couch in a club. I had a burning desire to help others. In my mind-at the time-, the only way I could achieve that version of success was with money and a lot of it. I knew I could not live the life I wanted by just going to school and getting the same degree everyone else has just to go wait in line for my name to be called at some pointless job. I honestly have no interest in that anyway. To go get a job and still be living paycheck to paycheck, to have to ask permission to take a day off, to have to ask for permission to spend time with my future children or go on a vacation was nothing I wanted to involve myself in.

Growing up these were all thoughts that I had in my head. In some situations, the life described above works for people, and some can live a very comfortable life as a result. However, as I just stated, my vision of success was different. I knew for a fact football could give me all that I wanted out of life. My greatest fear at this point in my life, and from the time I was young, was not making it to the NFL and letting myself and my family down. I honestly did not have any other avenue available that I felt I would be able to go into and live the life that I intended on living. This fear ultimately pushed me. When I was 18 and in junior college, I wrote my mother a letter because I couldn't get her a gift for her birthday. The letter said, "In a couple of years you won't have to worry about anything." Well, it was a couple years later, and my mother was still not in a place I knew she truly wanted to be deep-down inside; that was a hard pill to swallow. I knew for a fact if I made it to the NFL a lot of stuff would be different, and my mother would be able to live out her dream. Therefore, I mistakenly put a lot of blame on myself.

CHAPTER FOUR

IDENTIFY THEFT

P robably the most detrimental aspect of pouring every single ounce of oneself into the sport is the fact that we may lose sight of who we truly are. In my experience through my years of playing football from Pop Warner, to high school, to college, to the lower ranks of professional leagues-I can say that as a player your identity is or can be forced upon you in a sense: I was consumed by football to such a large degree that, figuratively speaking, when I reflect on the past, football clothed me every day. Once I felt like it was over and football was cut from me as a player, I felt naked. It felt like many of my insecurities were creeping back into my mind-back into my life.

To transition into the next phase of our lives, which we know will be vastly different from the past several years, we need to seek out our identity. In my college years I recall making the statement, "Football is something I love doing; it does not define me. I am more than someone who plays football." At that current time, I truly believed that no matter how much time I invested into the sport, no matter how much I loved it, it did not define me as a person or make up my entire identity. A couple of years later I would come to see that statement as being false. I guess I was lying to myself the whole time. I never realized, throughout my middle school years all the way through college and my very brief stint at striving to make it in the professional ranks, that football was in fact my identity. From my middle school years up until I decided to move on from the sport, everything I did was football or related to football in some fashion. I never really knew who I was as an individual. Everything I was, came from me playing football: my friends, my college degree, my relationship with my father. Therefore, as I got older, I began to worry that when I moved on, I would be moving on from other aspects of my life as well, specifically my father. As soon as I was finished playing, I worried that our relationship would suffer because I was not playing football anymore. I questioned if my father was only interested in my life because I was playing football. Deep down I told myself that it would not matter. However, something inside me believed that our relationship would in fact change.

My mother and father divorced when I was very young; as a result, my older brother and I would travel from Virginia to visit him in New York over the summers. Through the years, it seemed that football was the one thing that centered our relationship. It was the magnetic force that brought us together. However, when I was finished playing football for good, two or three phone calls a week, sometimes more, soon turned into a phone call maybe every two weeks, maybe even further apart, and there were sporadic text messages as well. Football was so much my identity, that maybe the phone calls digressed since my father did not even know what the topic of conversation would be if we spoke. All this was the result of the identity I formed being stripped away from me. It simply hindered our father-son relationship. Who is to blame for that, is it myself or my Father? Is it being both of us? Or maybe it is society, who puts so much praise on young kids to make it to the NFL, displaying them as gods to the world, while the failures are left feeling like they have no worth.

Throughout my three years in middle school I was the victim of a lot of bullying. It was the worst three years of my life. It was also the beginning of being given an identity that allowed me to gain some sense of confidence and security, apart from my family. I looked different than your "typical" young African American; for one thing my hair was straight like a white boy. I was smaller compared to all my peers, many who were bigger because they were behind a grade or two. My years in middle school drastically altered my ability to socialize with others, totally killing any ounce of confidence I previously possessed. This experience handicapped me years down the line. I absolutely hated school and hated myself. I hated my appearance; I did not feel accepted. For the eight hours within school, I felt useless; I felt I had no true friends. There were times I had to hold back tears in the middle of class. My temper increased causing me to lash out on others or get into a fight. I began to just hate people in general. The only time that I felt secure in myself was when I was home with my family or playing a sport. Once I stepped foot on the bus to head to school, I would try and sink low in my seat and be as quiet as a mouse. I never wanted to attract any kind of attention towards myself, whether good or bad. Every day I would go into school praying that nobody had anything to say to me or even notice me. I can probably count on one hand the number of days I went to school and was not picked on. I was called a terrorist an immigrant, a wetback. The teasing was horrible to the point I started asking myself "am I adopted?" It messed with me mentally on so many levels, instilling in me the need to create some type of identity for myself. I began to question if I am who people said I was. I never opened my mouth and voiced my thoughts to my family, but, within my head, I would question if this was my real family. Is my mother really my mother? I know we look alike but maybe that is just from spending everyday together. No one said my brother and I looked like we are brothers, so these doubts became more believable. From my dad to my cousins, I began to believe they were not my true family. All of this came from being a victim of bullying. When I would get home after school to my grandma's house I would go upstairs, and cry and ask God, "Why is this happening to me? Why do people have to be so hateful?"

Thankfully, football became my outlet from all that I was going through. As a kid, I wanted to be accepted by my peers, and in my mind, the only way that I could achieve acceptance was through sports. I knew I had some talent; all I did in the neighborhood was play basketball and football every single day with my friends. When I was 12 years old going towards the end of my 7th grade year I began to formulate an identity for myself. From May through the beginning of June, I got involved in a football camp for player development in my community, We actually practiced at my middle school; funny how the place I dreaded to go to in the morning became a place I could not wait to get to in the evening. Knowing that some of the kids who would bully me during school were at the same camp, I knew I could take advantage of this new environment. If I could dominate them for the 2 hours, then I would be fine.

The program was called Junior Player Development, which is a well-known organization throughout the country. It was there that my attitude toward football changed. I had loved the game from the time I was seven years old, but I hadn't thought of it as a way to map out my dreams. During this program, I started to believe football would make my dreams come true; it triggered something in my mind to give the game everything I could, every day of my life.

When I arrived on the first day, I did not know which team I was going to be a part of. That is until a coach who I played against in a basketball league saw me and quickly pulled me over to his team, the Bengal's. Over the course of the first week of camp, the team ended up being split up into two teams, and I ended up on the Cowboys; this resulted in my playing the next three football seasons with them. I believe it was God's work that I got sent to Coach Tony, a well-known coach in the area. He is a great coach and an even better husband to his wife and father to his children; not to mention, a great role model to the countless number of young males he impacted greatly through their childhood years and up until this very day. Even though I am in my 20's, Coach Tony has remained an important voice to me; even though we don't talk as much as we used to, I still keep the words he told me close to my heart. He always instilled in us the importance of working hard at anything we do and treating others with respect. He was also one of the few coaches that I genuinely felt cared about what we did off the field more than what we could do on the field. It annoyed me in a sense, how much emphasis he would put on finding other things I like to do outside of football. He would always ask us about the type of career we would like to involve ourselves in down the line. I should have taken his advice; however, due to my obsession with the game, I felt that he did not believe in my ability to make it to the NFL. In retrospect this was very stubborn of me. I believe, sometimes as athletes, we allow our pride to block our blessings. Sometimes we choose to block out the voices of those that may have our best interest at heart-beyond football. We can be so stuck on making it big that we tune out other opportunities, which we have the potential to love just as much as football. Although he was only doing his best to make sure I was successful when I finished playing, I foolishly let it go in one ear and out the other. Now, I am grateful for his advice.

Within the first week of camp, I missed a Wednesday night practice, since at the time I regularly attended a Wednesday night youth group at my church. This caused a conflict, as I was planning on being the starting quarterback for the upcoming season. Coach Tony pulled me to the side and told me if I want to play quarterback for his team, I was going to have to choose between Bible study and football. Now he is a man of faith; therefore, he was not against me going to church; he just knew that certain sacrifices would need to be made. He also told me that I needed throw every day and continuously work on my footwork to be his quarterback. To be in the competition for the starting quarterback spot, I convinced my mother to allow me to skip Bible study and attend practice. She allowed me to make the ultimate decision. I began to miss church on Wednesdays because of the burning desire I had to play football and the joy I received from playing the game.

Overall this provided a place for me to have peace and solitude from the bullying I was experiencing. Couple my treatment at school with the fact that my father was overseas fighting in the Iraq war, and anyone can see it was very difficult to deal with. It was especially hard-to be called a "terrorist" and "Afghan" while my dad was going to war everyday against those people. Almost every night I cried myself to sleep not knowing if I was going to wake up to news that my father was killed. During that time, football had the ability to put me in a totally different world; it was a place where I felt accepted, and I was slowly forming my identity within the game. At that moment in my life, I felt more peace on the football field than I did in a church. I still felt that I did not belong sometimes, so I spent as much time involved with football as I possibly could. As I became better at the quarterback position, my confidence began to build up in my life. My self-esteem rose-all from the sport of football.

After reaching the National Championship tournament at the University of Arizona in the beginning of December and winning it all, I truly felt I had the potential to mold myself into an NFL player based off how I performed. Once I returned to school, I was able to walk the halls with my head and chest held just a little bit higher. I was in love with the feeling, in love with the identity football was forming in me-even if I did not notice it at the time. It felt like I had a superpower; one that began to prevent much of the bullying, and I never wanted this power to dissipate. I felt that some of my classmates began to look at me a little different when they realized I had talent and was blessed enough to travel to play football.

Without football, I do not know where I would have ended up, especially in my younger years. However, years later I found myself questioning if maybe I would have been in a better place without football being in my life. Football helped get me through the personally tough times of my childhood, which I will be forever grateful for. I did not have all the friends that people would naturally think an athlete would have, especially a quarterback, but I always had football. Now as a 23-year-old young man moving on from football, that identity was no longer there to give me that security blanket I had grown so used to. I felt like I was lost in life. When I was upset, frustrated, or angry as a kid I could just go work on my game for as long as I wanted-always working with the vision in my head of making it to the NFL. Now the game was not there, and the goal was absent from my life. I needed to lean on my faith, my family, and my loved ones to help get me over the hump. I needed to reinvent myself and seek the identity that God had given me, I needed to seek God and allow his work to take place in my life however he saw fit. Early on, I chose not to do that.

CHAPTER FIVE

LAST CHANCE U

When it came to high school ball I ended up only playing one season, my senior season. I continued to play two more seasons of league ball with Coach Tony, my ninth and tenth grade years, going to two more National Championships. I remained in league play because I enjoyed it a lot and my high school was terrible in football to say the least. Also, since the father of one of the other quarterbacks on the high school team was the quarterback coach, and the fact I suffered an injury during my junior year, I only played in nine full games throughout high school. I did not even play a full season, and I ended up missing the last game of my senior year due to academic ineligibility. School was just something I did not care for; all I wanted to do was play football. Despite a lack of playing time on the high school gridiron, I had some interest from colleges. My coach had me slated for the Division IAA level, but even if I was blessed to receive a Division I or Division IAA scholarship, I still was not academically eligible.

It worked out for me in the end, as I still needed some time to develop my game. With a Division I or Division IAA school now out of the picture, the only option for me was to attend a junior college, since I did not want to attend a Division II school out of high school. Junior College (JUCO) football presented a good opportunity for a kid like me to right his wrongs and mature a little more before having the chance to enroll into a four-year university. It also affords a player the opportunity to develop their game. But I never even heard of JUCO until one of my teammates who was a year ahead of me went that route after high school. He ended up receiving a scholarship to Kansas University and eventually went on to the Chicago Bears rookie camp. When he first told me about it, my first response was, "nah I'm not going to no JUCO, what is that!?" However, after doing some research and listening to my head coach's take on it, since he played at Jones JUCO in Mississippi and had the opportunity to play at Division IAA Elon University, I realized that this was another avenue I could take to reach my goal of making it to the Division I level. A JUCO could be used as a steppingstone and place to develop my game. But there were so many options.

I had to decide between New Mexico Military Institute (NMMI) in Roswell, Merced College in California and East Central in Mississippi. Ultimately, I went with the New Mexico route. Man talk about culture shock! This was the first time I saw a tumble weed. I felt like I was in a cartoon or some wild-wild-west movie stranded in the desert. Plus, this was in the city of Roswell where they believe aliens landed; safe to say operation "get out of dodge" was in full effect. Especially when the first thing they did to us was shave our heads, which we had no clue that was going to happen. But I was already there and could not go back, so I did my best to get the most out of the experience that I could. NMMI wasn't your typical JUCO, like you see on *Last Chance U,* due to it being centered around a very strict, military structure. So, a lot of time away from football was spent doing other activities, like marching in the grass at 4am and walking around in the Army Combat Uniform (ACU) all day. Some of us African American athletes even experienced some racism. What an experience. Also, there was not too much down time to talk with my teammates outside of practice; I mean we couldn't even talk at breakfast, lunch, or dinner. Despite the lack of a social life, my main goal going in was football. On the football end of things, I went in intending to get the starting spot; however, I was beat out by another kid who was pretty good in his own right. I thought we were pretty much neck and neck, but he was from the city of Roswell, so maybe that hometown advantage gave him the edge. Though I didn't get what I set out to, I did not have time to pout. I remained a good teammate and knew in the back of my head that I would not be sitting on the bench the whole season.

Shortly before our first game, the offensive coordinator created a wildcat package for me, which I thought was pretty dope. This was in 2010, when every team in America it seemed was implementing the wildcat package into their offense. My first time touching the ball in college was picture perfect to say the least. I got the shotgun snap, darted up the middle, and bounced it outside for a ninety-one-yard touchdown. I never thought of that happening, but it felt amazing! From that point on, I figured I could still make an impact that season starting position or not. After that game, the coaches decided to move me to kick return, as well as increase the wildcat package. As the season progressed, I was able to make some impact plays with what I was given. Off the field, however, I began to get into conflict with the school and how it operated outside of football. I, unfortunately, ended up not being able to travel with the team the last few weeks of the season. I questioned if I should even stay at the school, even after the head coach tried to convince me to stay and play corner for him. He told me I could develop into a top-flight Division I corner. I did not know how I felt about all that at the time, so I decided to look for a way to transfer to another JUCO and play quarterback.

I received a scholarship to ASA Junior College in Brooklyn, NY. That is where I experienced the real side of JUCO football. I don't think it is a coincidence that one of the better series on Netflix, with regards to football, is called "Last Chance U." At least, that is my opinion. I am sure that many people who will pick up this book have seen or at least heard of this series that depicts the raw, uncut and unfiltered life of JUCO football. For those who are unfamiliar with JUCO, it is a dog eat dog world, which I kind of liked. It meant that I could not slack or take a day off. Every player is there with one goal in mind, to go D-I and make it to the NFL-nothing more nothing less. School was not high on the list of priorities for many of us. The living conditions are not always the best either. My room had four of us staying in there. Food was often scarce, since we didn't have any meal plans. Thank God my family is from New York, so I helped teammates out where I could with food. We all were willing to deal with it because we knew that the slim chance of any of us making it to the league sounded sweeter than dealing with the fact that we would probably be lost in our own respective ways without the game. Those are the sacrifices that come with JUCO. In JUCO the competition is intense, and you had to bring your a-game every single day because the person behind you, in most cases, wants to get out of that JUCO and go to a four-year university. Just like you, everyone is there fighting for their life-figuratively and literally. It was an intense atmosphere; any given practice a player may get into a fist fight with one of the coaches or someone might literally get kicked off the team for leaning on equipment in the weight room. JUCO was not a place where anything was going to come easy, so every day I worked as if it was my last chance. It's like there was a sense of fear in the majority of us on the team, especially the second-year guys approaching the timeframe where it's time to move on from JUCO to a four year-university. In the back of your head is the thought "what if it doesn't work? What if I don't get a scholarship" It was the last chance for all of us, honestly. For a lot of guys, if they do not make it out of JUCO then that is the end of the road for them. It's more than the last chance at football, it is possibly the last chance at a life they want and have planned for.

As I look back on my stay in junior college and reflect on the time I spent with some of the "bounce backs," I can make some general observations. For those that do not know what a "bounce back" is; it describes a player who goes to a four-year university and ends up being removed from the university for academic issues, behavioral issues, desire to change divisions, etc. This results in them landing at a JUCO.

My first observation is that the NCAA fails the student athletes by not putting a huge emphasis on their development as an individual, which causes them to fail at their four-year universities. My second observation is the general attitude within some student athletes I noticed. It is evident that some have no plans to change their ways, which is why they get kicked out of their DI school.

Now, as I stated above, some fault lies within the athletes themselves. However, if you take an 18-year-old from home to attend a prestigious university, you would think that they would be able to better themselves as an individual while attending the university. The majority of "bounce backs" I was around stated that, while at their previous school there was not a major emphasis on bettering them as a person. Keep in mind many D-I and D-II schools with a large football program bring athletes in to be a part of a team whose goal is to win football games and bring more revenue in. MAYBE they will help players make it to the league. Once these players arrive at the JUCO level, they are supposed to get a wake-up call, a chance to humble themselves and make a huge change in their lives.

It does not make much sense to me why the number one option of a disgruntled student athlete is to be sent to JUCO to change. The last time I checked, a teammate never told me they were purposely removed due to them not being a good athlete. It was always along the lines of behavioral issues. I do not know about every JUCO in the country but at my JUCO there was no outlet for that bounce back to correct their behavior. There was just ample time to become better at football. Therefore, you often hear about players going to a JUCO, only to return to a university and be removed again. Maybe the kid has mental issues, or maybe it is a psychological component causing the kid to be deviant. So, the solution from the NCAA is to send them to a JUCO where football is being filled with kids who lack discipline, structure, stable homes, academic issues, and much more? Honestly, what do you really expect to happen when the psychological and mental health of the athlete is being neglected? Some coaches can make a major impact on a student athlete at the JUCO level. However, when it comes down to it, the coach is trying to win games and move up just like everyone else. Therefore, there is not a tremendous amount of time allotted towards helping the student athlete develop his skills off the playing field. There should be professionals in the field of mental health employed by the schools, whose sole focus is to enhance the mental aspect of the athlete while at their respective JUCO.

For those who are familiar with "Last Chance U," you saw how East Mississippi Community College had somebody in place, Ms. Wagner, to truly try and combat the academic and behavioral issues that the athletes faced. Ms. Pinkard at Independence Community College served in the same role. It was cool to see that even after the players left the school, Ms. Wagner kept in touch with them and made them feel important; she tries to show them that their life holds purpose beyond football. As athletes, having something like that in place at the JUCO level is only successful when we meet those that support us halfway. We see positive results only if we take advantage of people who are willing to work with us and help us become successful, instead of blowing them off and putting all our focus only on football.

To successfully maneuver through the junior college route where there are so many distractions you truly must have an extreme amount of discipline and focus. At that level there is a high turnover rate. When I was at ASA, it felt like they would be bringing in a new player on a weekly basis, and within that same week that same player could be right back on the bus heading home. Everyone there is looking to move up, so that "every man" for himself mentality is prevalent, and you are compelled to worry only about yourself at the end of the day. However, while focusing on yourself, it is so important that you surround yourself with teammates that are like minded. We are all smart enough to know who to spend our time with and who not to. I was blessed to have roommates that were just as focused as I was to make it to the next level, and there were other teammates that I hung with as well. When times get tough, which they will at the JUCO level, you will need positive people around you to pull you up. From then until now, I still talk with one of my JUCO roommates. It helps having positive people stay the course with you throughout your journey. We used to talk about football all the time at ASA; now we send insightful information on real estate, mindset, and finances-among other things. I cannot emphasize enough how spending my time with positive influences and talking about our goals together helped propel us to be able to receive scholarships and successfully move on to our four-year universities.

My 3 roommates signed with Wagner, Arkansas Pine Bluff, and Houston-with one making it into the NFL. I had generated some small interest from some D-I programs, and my quarterback coach, who played at Villanova, tried to get me in, but they had a sudden coaching staff change. Any chance I had to attend there quickly fell through. I knew I had a chance at possibly getting to a Division I school; however, I decided to head to Bowie State, a Division II school, in December of 2012. I would have had to wait to graduate in May in order to attend a D-I. Who knows if I had decided to stick it out until May, maybe I would have made good on my D-I dream? But I honestly was ready to get out of there and play football, and where I played did not matter to me anymore. The decision to choose a D-II university has played in my mind frequently, but at the time, I had to just give my all to my university and let the chips fall where they may.

CHAPTER SIX

LEAGUE DREAMS

My time spent at Bowie State did not go how I would ideally like it to go, on the field that is. I put a lot of pressure on myself to be successful and have a career that would propel me into the professional ranks. With some of the success that I did achieve; I think that I hindered my chances at reaching more success from being overly focused on being perfect on the field, not wanting to fail, instead of truly having fun playing the game. Every single pass had to be 100% accurate, every single drop back had to be precise; if not, I felt that would be a chink in my armor. I feared that I would end up being benched as a result, ultimately missing out on my chance at the pros. This was especially true during my first season at Bowie.

It got started off great, like a dream. I honestly could not have drawn up my first home game going any better. It was a tough fought game. We rallied from a fourteen-point deficit, gaining the lead late in the fourth quarter, yet to end up being down 20-17 with just thirty-three seconds left in the game. Every quarterback dreams of this moment, being down with little time left on the clock and a chance to make your mark. We ended up driving sixty-five yards on four plays. With five seconds left, I got the shotgun snap and threw a fade route to our top receiver and he came down with it, game over! I finished the game with 274 yards passing and three passing touchdowns. The feeling was amazing, I envisioned building on this momentum and having a great season.

The next week I felt like the man walking on campus, I told myself I could get used to this for sure. To cap it off, we had a national televised game coming up on Thursday night against Benedict College in Columbia, South Carolina. This game was the DII game of the week, being broadcasted on CBS Sports Network. This was my first opportunity to play on National television. It came with a few butterflies, but nothing that was to unfamiliar, once the first play is over it's just football. However, on the second play, I took the shotgun snap on a zone read and darted to the left where I was met by a defender, I spun away from him and immediately was struck head on by the safety; it was one of the hardest head to head hits that I experienced. I was able to get up and gather myself. I knew something was wrong when I looked to the sideline for the play but could not identify all the play signals. About two more plays went by and I began to recite the play calling verbiage from ASA inside the huddle, "timeout, timeout" I had to walk off the field and ended up being diagnosed with a concussion on the sideline.

Thankfully we still came out on top in the game. The concussion resulted in me missing our next game, which we won, and our backup quarterback played a hell of a game. When the following week came, I was still the starting quarterback, but something was off about me. I didn't play as well and ended up getting in a rotating quarterback situation for the remainder of the season. I begin playing the game with some restrictions. I didn't feel to confident in my solidity as the starting quarterback, knowing I had to constantly look over my shoulder making sure I don't make a mistake and possibly have my playing time taken away.

My second season at Bowie State took a major shift. We had a new offensive coordinator, which resulted in our offense opening up a lot more. We were previously a run first team, however a new mind on the offensive side challenged that philosophy and allowed our offense to expand, which led to some good things as an offense.

Now fast forward towards the end of my senior season in college.

I had no teams coming to see me, and I was not on anybody's draft board. Coming from Bowie State, a Division II university, there is much more that a quarterback must achieve to get a look from NFL scouts. I had broken a few records; however, I did not have the eye-popping numbers to attract NFL scouts, nor did my team have a record that would warrant scouts to even take a glance our way. I was honest with myself, and I was aware of the reality of my situation. Despite this, I knew that I had the talent to get an opportunity.

Two players from Bowie had recently made it to the NFL, and I also played with a wide receiver who would eventually have high success in the AFL and get his shot at the NFL, and a tight end who is still in the NFL to this day. On top of that I had heard of numerous players who came out of nowhere, going from unknown to a household name. All of this gave me hope. I knew that I still wanted to reach my dream no matter what my current situation was at the time. My head coach had told my mother that he believed I was the best athlete in the CIAA, the conference that I was playing in, and knowing that I figured "Ok, hopefully, I can have a shot with a CFL or AFL team to start out."

That did not happen. I'm not pointing the finger at anyone. Maybe I did not do my best at displaying my talent to the fullest. My offensive coordinator mentioned that if it was in his hands, he would have done his best to help me out. I just had to decide what choices to make after my senior year in order to still pursue my dreams. So, I began to seek out other avenues that could possibly give me some type of exposure.

For spring break of my senior year, I went down to Georgia to visit my dad for the week; he had been living there for about two years. He mentioned that there was a facility named Georgia Sports Performance (GSP) near him that trained NFL players, as well as prepared college players for their Pro Days or for the combine and many other athletes of varying age groups. I visited, and I was able to meet with the owner, who was a quarterback coach. We were able to get some good work in, and I learned a few tips that I felt would help my game, as I was still pursuing my dream of becoming a professional quarterback. While there, one of the trainers, Eric Johnson, -who played with the Raiders in the NFL for several years-was the head defensive backs coach and speed coach. He was constantly putting a bug in my ear about possibly giving the corner position a shot. All this came though he had never even seen me do a backpedal or come out of my break, so I was a little thrown off and skeptical about it; however, he did have years of experience in the NFL. I began to seriously consider this switch, as this was not the first time a coach told me I should consider moving to corner. This was not due to me being incapable of playing quarterback. I guess they just felt my skills would adapt to the corner position more effectively. I gave it some thought but never dwelled on it too much.

The thing about being in a training facility like this, which welcomed NFL players, is that you never know who you would run into or who would be watching from a distance. It just so happened that the Atlanta Falcons' Director of Player Personal's son, who was in high school, trained at the same facility. One day, during that week while I was on the field in the middle of a training session doing some field drills and sprint work, the Director of Player Personal was standing with my dad and another guy, and he did not know that my dad was in fact my dad-at the time. He spoke about me just based off his first impression and said, "Man, who is that kid!?" After my workout while changing my shoes getting ready to leave, I sensed somebody approaching me. Low and behold, it was the Director of Player Personal. I looked up, and he was standing right over me. He introduced himself and asked my name, what school I went to, and when my Pro Day was. I stood up and introduced myself, told him that I played quarterback and that I attended Bowie State University; however, I could not inform him of a Pro Day due to my school not having one. At that time, I was still holding out to play quarterback. When my career dreams ended, I used to wish I didn't and wondered if the meeting had happened a half year later, once I trained to play corner, he would have thought differently as the height of 6'1 would have made more of an impression, compared to a 6'1 quarterback. Either way, there was no Pro Day so it did not matter. This did serve as another boost for my confidence though. Like man! A Falcons staff member approached me out of the blue! Ok! I know I really can do this!

Once I returned to school, I had a few weeks before the NFL regional combine at the Baltimore Ravens facility. I performed well and was interviewed after being identified as one of the top performing quarterbacks at the combine. I knew that did not mean much, as far as a team possibly noticing me and giving me some type of shot. However, it was the glimmer of hope that I needed at the time.

Once the NFL draft came around, it hurt knowing that I had worked diligently and relentlessly for so many years to have an opportunity to hear my name called, but there was no being selected selected by a team, no phone call inviting me to camp. There was only the feeling of ultimately coming up short of my lifelong dream. This felt like my first true failure. Of course, in my life up until this point I had failed at things, but as far as failing at something I was passionate about, this was a first. I was kind of just stuck for a while, as if time was now at a standstill.

I decided to not even pursue football anymore. It was not because I was just through with the sport, but I was just so confused as to what to do and what would come next. It seemed that it was best for me to separate myself from the game. I finished up that spring semester-going to class with no motivation at all and constantly pondering my future. I began to not even want to graduate, because I knew I would have to face the real world. I knew that I was not fully ready, and to make things worse, I was facing the very likely possibility that I would get a job where I would be bored. I was very depressed. I was coming to the realization that it may be time to move on to something else in my life. The issue was I had absolutely no idea of what that something else would even be. Ultimately, the struggle with me deciding what I wanted to do led to me slacking in a class, which forced me to stay until the following fall semester. With my scholarship running out, graduating late, and accumulating a little bit of college debt, I was still not prepared to make the necessary transition, and I began to let fear consume me. As much as I tried to hide that I was in a state of confusion, the feelings would surface when I would be alone in my dorm room, and I began to think about being successful. I still wanted to achieve my dreams for my life: be able to live a great life, be financially stable, and be able to live life to the fullest. At the time, I could not picture that being something that I would accomplish in my life. Football was and always had been the window in which I could look through and see everything being alright. At that moment, it felt as if the blinds had been shut on me.

I returned, as I said before, for one more fall semester, which was of course during the football season. Seeing my former teammates walking to practice or rushing to meetings made me miss it more. It made it difficult to even attend the football games. I felt like I was out of place. Now I had fun with my friends, which kept me smiling and made me feel like a "regular" college kid. Other than that, I felt I had no purpose being in school. This was the first time I felt that there was no definite purpose in me attending college. There was nothing to look forward to. In all my past college years I was on a schedule. After class, I knew for a fact I had practice during the season; sometimes they were before classes, at the crack of dawn. In the offseason I knew when I woke up, I had 5 am workouts to go to, I had meetings in the afternoon, or I had 7 on 7 sessions. If we did not have anything to do or little to do on a particular day, then I was doing something on my own to get me prepared for the season. This was the first time in my college career that I did not engage in consistent action to achieve anything football related. I began soul-searching. It took me a few months to come to a decision, but I finally decided what I want to do with the next phase of my life after graduation.

One last shot

. . .

It was not until December of 2014, right before graduation, that I had decided to give football one more shot. I decided to go back down south after graduation to give it my all and see where the chips would fall. I was at the point where I was going to either move on or continue to chase my dream. My head coach told me if I wanted to continue to pursue football then I should give it a solid year and see what comes out of it. I felt like I had more in the tank, a lot more. I felt that I was still young at 22 years old and had a lot to offer an organization, whether it be the NFL, CFL or AFL. One thing that I always promised myself is that I would always be real with myself, no matter what. For example, if I knew I did not have a legitimate shot or that my talent level was no longer at a competitive level then I would decide to move on. I truly believed in my heart that I would go down to Georgia and be picked up by a professional organization. Did I go there saying I am going straight to the NFL? No. However I knew I had the talent level to have a chance. My goal was to go there and become a part of an AFL or CFL team and work my way up, which I had no issue with I was used to the hard work and having to prove myself once again.

So close

. . .

I felt I was very close to achieving my dreams once I got to Georgia. When I say I felt the closest to my dream, I am referring to the fact that I was training with current NFL players daily. They looked just like me, walked like me, and talked like me. After seeing them firsthand, I was like "Ohhh man! Let's go! I have everything they could possibly want! I can run and jump. I have the talent; I have the skill. I have the intelligence, the athleticism, the work ethic, and the commitment!" However, God had other plans for me: plans which I did not agree with.

I spent about 6 months in Georgia training for an opportunity with a NFL, CFL, or AFL team, and, after thinking about what would grant me the best opportunity, I decided to make the change to defensive back. With the memories of college coaches stopping by my high school and asking me to play defensive back and the memories at JUCO when my coach made the pitch about being a cornerback, I began to train. I knew if given the right opportunity and if I performed to the best of my abilities, I would capitalize on the opportunity that was given. I received only praise from trainers and college athletes, as well as the NFL players. One athlete played on the Tampa Bay Buccaneers, and almost every day he would say to me, "Man, all you need is a workout with a team, and you're straight." There would be D-I coaches that would come watch some of the top high school guys. I remember one day an FIU coach saw me at some point on the field and inquired with the owner of the gym about me. He did not know I had just graduated college, and while I could not do anything for his team, this inquiry was another indicator that I know I had what it takes.

Guys that played at Georgia-in arguably the best college football conference in the country-were saying "Man I done been around a lot of good athletes-you got it! Keep working!" I knew I had what it took but hearing it from others who played at the higher level added to the faith I already had in myself.

Being able to train beside Josh Norman, who is arguably one of the best cornerbacks in the NFL, was really eye opening for me. He is a great football player and a great person above all. I was able to pick up on some of the techniques I saw him utilize, and I used him as a measuring stick for my own skills. Everything he could do; I could do the same. It blew my mind when I saw he signed that huge contract with the Redskins, which he deserved. I just knew that I could do the same thing. It felt like I could just touch my dream!

CHAPTER SEVEN

PRO BALL

While I was in Georgia training I attended a couple of CFL tryouts. One that I attended was for the Edmonton Eskimos, in which I tried out for defensive back. I knew that not having film as a defensive back, I would need to find a way to attract the coach's attention beforehand, so he would have an idea about me by the time the tryout started. Where I was training at, we would have "mock Pro Days" doing all the various combine drills. I was running consistent forties at 4.5 seconds; my vertical was 37.5 inches, and I was constantly getting 3.98 seconds in the 20-yard short shuttle. All this was complimented by my 6'1 and right under 200-pound frame. I knew those numbers could at least garner the attention of-somebody important. Due to head coach of the Edmonton Eskimos being close to a trainer at the gym, he heard about my numbers and my size and was intrigued. I knew that did not mean I would be selected to join the team. It only meant that I would have a better chance at being closely watched. Now, the few CFL tryouts that I had been to before this one had hundreds of athletes trying out, which is the downside of the CFL tryouts in my opinion. Because of this, it is best to already be on the team's radar, so you get your monies worth. Honestly, it can be a waste of your time and money if you aren't-unless you plan on running a 4.2 forty. With that many in attendance, it can be difficult to get noticed, depending on your position. This tryout, however, had maybe thirty participants. Once

I introduced myself to the head coach, he instantly knew who I was from his previous conversations with the trainer at the gym. I told myself this was the perfect situation. All I needed to do was show out.

Once it got to the combine drills, I lined up to do my short shuttle. As soon as I made my first move out of my stance, I felt a pull in my hip and groin area and went down to my knees. It was a reoccurring injury that I had played through all my seasons at Bowie State. There were times where it hurt just to walk, and I was in the training room almost every day for treatment. I never was given a true diagnostic of the injury. I just thought "man this was the most unfortunate time. Why would this happen now!?" However, I knew that was just another minor setback. Even though I missed out on a potentially great opportunity, I knew in a couple of days I would be able to manage.

Now or Never

. . .

In the following month I had a tryout to attend with the Columbus Lions of the Professional Indoor Football League (PIFL), in Columbus GA. The indoor game is slightly different than the AFL, and it is a step below. There are different rules, which are very minimal, but other than that it is played in the same type of venue as the AFL. This was not what I had planned for when I decided to come to Georgia to pursue my dream. Although this was not the NFL, CFL, or AFL, the Lions were a dominant team in their league and had won multiple championships. They even sent a few players off to the AFL and CFL. I was a little disappointed when the defensive back coach from the training facility told me I should go; I had always had my hopes set higher than that. However, at the end of the day, knowing my situation, I had to take the first opportunity that presented itself, and this one seemed to be a solid one. I had to be real with myself and realize that this was the only opportunity I had now, and I needed to take it and make the best out of it.

This tryout was towards the end of their season, so anyone who made the team would be brought in the following season. Honestly though, you coming back hinged on whether they still wanted you by the start of the next season; it's just the way the game goes. Before the tryout I had spoken with one of the owners of the team. He called to inform me of the process and what to do when we arrived at the stadium. I could tell that this was just a money grabber-an attempt by a team to get money from tryouts without having any real expectations for players to make the team. This rubbed me the wrong way. In my mind, I felt that they should not compare me or categorize me with anybody else. I put the work in; I grinded every day, and I knew I had the skills to be competitive for their team. I felt disrespected, so this gave me added fuel, which I did not need in the first place. But I welcomed it with open arms and accepted the challenge.

Once the day of the tryout came and we got on the field, I knew I was the best athlete out there-hands down. The tryout went well, and I did what I was supposed to do. I truly felt that I proved my ability well enough to get a spot on the team. I displayed that I was athletic, skilled, and coachable. At the end of the tryout, they began calling each person back to the locker room one by one, to inform us of their decision. Everyone, for the most part came back with bad news. A few came back extremely happy because they got invited to camp in the spring. They took forever to call me back, and the wait just made me more and more anxious. I ended up being the last one called. I guess they decided to save the best for last. On my walk to the locker room I was nervous, just saying to myself "I hope I made it. I hope I made it." I was thinking that if this opportunity did not pan out for me then maybe I would try to move on-even though that was the last thing I wanted. Thankfully, I was told they were bringing me on immediately! I was so focused and determined, I did not even smile when they told me. Now, I knew there was so much more that needed to be done. Eventually, the coaches did get me to smile. They told me I would have another tryout in a sense. I had two days to practice with the team, and they would decide from there. I felt so happy that, finally, my hard work was paying off. I immediately called my mother to tell her the good news; it felt amazing and was a huge relief at the moment. This was not the NFL; however, in my situation it was just what I needed. Having not played defensive back in college, I knew I could use this opportunity to get good film and get exposure from being with an organization that had proven that they could send guys up the professional ranks with ease. I already knew they were going to like me once they saw me in practice, so I was not worried about staying on after my two days were completed. I already planted in my head that I was not going back up to my father's house after these two days. It was now or never in my mind.

Thankfully, I ended up staying with the team for the last month and a half or so of the season. I received, no pay, but that shows how bad I wanted it. I was blessed to have either my mom or my father send me some money here and there, which I used strictly for food and nothing else. I was willing to deal with delayed gratification, because I felt my situation was temporary and I would get a return on my time invested. I was able to learn the arena game and really enhance my level of play. I learned a lot from the older players, some of whom had played against top competition in the NFL, CFL, and AFL. It was a huge learning curve, but I came out of it very confident. I was eagerly waiting for my time to come.

As the weeks progressed, we ended up winning the championship. It felt good! Even though I did not get the chance to suit up, I just felt I was in the right place, and finally things began to look promising. Multiple teammates were blessed to move up the ranks to the AFL and start in the following season. Seeing them playing on TV only meant that I could well do the same. I was told by the coaches that next year was my time, and they felt I was more than ready after spending only a short time with the team. I just knew that it was my time.

Once I got back home to Virginia that summer, I had tunnel vision like never before. Now, I have always taken my craft serious, so seriously in fact that there are a few people in my life who I feel displayed the same dedication. The difference between my dedication in the past and that summer was that I could literally feel my dream coming true. I could taste it. In the meantime, I got a job at Nike in the mall by my house, and I worked at a dog kennel about 10 minutes from me. I saw both jobs as being temporary, and they gave me some pocket change to have. Better yet, they both still allowed me to focus and dedicate more time to getting ready for the upcoming season. Looking back, I could have taken a job that interested me a little more and that I would genuinely have enjoyed instead of working two jobs and not having the time to focus on myself. However, I was stuck on-achieving my goal. I remember doing drills while I was working at the kennel. We had a grass area outside the fences that I would clear of leaves. I knew nobody was going to come check on me, so I would get a little bit of football work in. I would work on my backpedal, coming out my breaks, etc. I didn't care where I was at; I was determined to get better every second possible. Every minute I could I was watching play-by-play of the best corners in the NFL, taking their techniques an implementing them into my game. I also studied top AFL defensive backs. All I could think about was how I was going to come into the season and become the undeniable best defensive back on the team, I set the goals that I wanted to achieve, and I was dialed in. I worked out every day. I had one of my old speed coaches train me in the gym, and everything else, as far as field work, I did on my own just like when I first started out. I never needed someone to force me to get up at 4 am to work out or to go run sprints at 8 pm. Mind you, the majority of the offseason it was freezing outside being that the season ended in the summer and started back up in the spring. Most of the time I would be getting my field work in freezing below 30-degree weather. A lot of the time I was out there at night, in the dark, because that was when I would have the entire filed to myself. Most people would have complained; however, I wanted it too bad to make up any type of excuse. I did not want to look back and regret anything or question if I had worked hard enough. I was filled with so much excitement, knowing I was moving one step forward towards my dream. So, after the months of hard work, it was time for me to drive down to Georgia for training camp. I knew that this was, quite frankly, my last opportunity to turn my dream into a reality, to make the promise to my mother come true, or at least make it one step closer.

CHAPTER EIGHT

TIME TO PROVE MYSELF

When I arrived back in Columbus, GA, I knew I had put all the work I could put in to make sure I was able establish myself as a starter and a top defensive back in the league. I was trying to position myself to move up to a higher level. I did everything any self-help book would tell you to do: I wrote my goals down and, I envisioned my success everyday leading up to camp-believing it would all manifest. It felt good arriving in the locker room on the first day and having all of our equipment and clothes laid out in the locker for us. We had our towels, soap, and lotion. They even had Gatorade, bananas, and chewy bars for us before each practice. We had free unlimited chiropractor treatments. Being with this organization felt amazing to me. It created a feeling of purpose and value in me, and I could only imagine how the treatment would be in the NFL. It made me even hungrier to arrive at that level. From the first day of camp, when we had to participate in our conditioning test, it was clear that I outworked every single player on that field during the-off season. I carried that performance into camp and easily displayed that I was a force to be reckoned with. At the time I was one of the youngest, if not the youngest, players on the team. We had a stacked team. I'm talking former 4- and 5-star athletes that played at FSU, UCLA, Oklahoma State, NC State, Stanford etc. There were also players that spent time in the NFL, and former CFL and top AFL players. We had it all. I knew I had some stiff competition ahead of me from the other defensive backs-three of which were previously in the NFL, and the two others who were older guys with a ton of experience from the CFL and AFL. Apart from our defense, we had some of the top receivers in the league to battle with each day; they could expose you if you did not show up. Clearly, I was the underdog, and I accepted my place with open arms. I had a chip on my shoulder and approached every practice as if it were a game. When I saw the talent level of the defensive backs that saw actual playing time in an NFL game, I knew I was better than them. It was easy for me to see, and it was evident to my coaches and teammates as well. I will give credit to one out of the three, who attended Northern Illinois and later played with the Tennessee Titans and the New York Jets. He was good and was good competition to go up against. However, after practicing and being around them every day, I honestly believed I had every single box checked off and knew that I could play in the NFL. I was at the least worthy enough to have a personal workout with a team. It was all about getting in front of the right eyes at this moment.

As training camp progressed compliments began to flood in from my teammates and the head coach. Coach Gibson, the head coach, approached me one day, while I was walking off of the practice field, and informed me how all of the players were raving to him about my ability to play and how much of an improvement they noticed from last season. This mostly came from the older guys, whose opinions he heavily considered. It got to the point where my roommate through training camp, who was from Miami, said to me one day after practice, "Man I ain't know you was that raw!" It felt good knowing that all my hard work was not going unnoticed. When you believe in your own ability and talents, that is a major plus. However, when others around you see it as well, you know it is real. I believed that I was on the right path, and the timing was perfect for me-as long as I stayed on top of my game.

As training camp progressed, I was getting better every day and continuing to improve my game. As cuts began to be made, I stayed focused on myself, and the number of defensive backs started to dwindle down. On the morning of one of our practices, before our second cut day, the head coach texted me saying to come to the facility at 9:45 am. I knew something was strange about that text as practice did not start until noon. On the drive over to the facility I was extremely nervous; I realized that I never knew when my last day would be. When I arrived, he talked to me one-on-one and told me that if I did not practice well that day then he was going to cut me- straight to the point. He stated that I had not improved. I knew it was complete BS, and he was playing the political game to try and have the former NFL players remain on the team. Two days before that-after the first cuts took place-he told me I am doing everything right, and if we had had a game that day I would have started. He had nothing negative to say, because I was dialed in all camp. I was highly pissed, but I had to just focus. I considered the possibility that he was saying that just to see if I would fold under the pressure. I went out to practice and did what I always did. I was blessed and did not get cut. After that practice, I just took a drive to clear my mind. The conversation and potential to get cut hurt me so much that I could not even drive. I had to pull into a parking lot and could not stop the tears from coming down. I was filled with so much anger; I was in disbelief that after all of the hard work I had put in and after showing that I belonged, I got told I may get cut. At that moment, I just felt the coach was toying with me. I kept my head down for the rest of camp and continued to stay on task.

By time the first game came around, I was named the fourth defensive back. The starting three were the two older experienced guys and Tracy who previously played for the Titans and Jets. I was happy, but nowhere near satisfied. I knew that I was not done; I was planning on taking one of their spots very soon. We ended up winning the first game, with all four of us playing in the game. Our opponents were horrible, to say the least, and we ended up scoring in the 90s. I saw very little time in the rotation but did play on the kickoff team, and I was able to get a tackle for a safety. I felt good after the game and was ready to roll into the next week and take the starting spot, as no spot was guaranteed week to week. However, it did not work out the way I envisioned it. I received a text from the head coach on the following Monday morning saying that I needed to come to his office and bring my play book. Anyone who has played football at the college or professional level knows that those words can cause your heart to drop. I remember saying over and over to myself "This man cannot be about to cut me!" When I arrived in his office, I sat down across from his desk with another coach in the office. They informed me that they were going to cut me to make room for an offensive lineman. Pure disappointment and betrayal is what I felt.. It hurt tremendously! I felt this had been the perfect opportunity for me. I tried my hardest to not show too much emotion, but it just hurt too bad. I could not help but tear up. The coach continued to tell me that he did not want to cut me, and he did not want to play against me. He began to tell me other teams in the PIFL that would be a good choice for me. It didn't make any sense to me: to go from singing my praises to sending me out the door when there were players who were not as good as me still on the team. Knowing that the guys that played in the NFL were still on the team and I was clearly the better football player provided me the reason to believe that I was cut was due to the politics of the game. Maybe I am wrong, but I doubt it. I kept my demeanor and thanked him for the chance, which I was genuinely thankful for. I drove back to the hotel to pack my things up and get ready to drive back to Virginia the following morning. At that point, I did not know what to think. I was still somewhat confused on how I could have worked so hard and proved to the coaching staff and the whole team that I belonged, just to end up getting cut.

While I was on the road back to Virginia the next morning, I got texts from one of my teammates saying how everyone on the team was shocked and knew it was some BS that happened. I accepted all the support, but it was still tough to deal with. It was a long, lonely ten-hour drive back home, and being cut made it seem even longer. It gave me a lot of time to think. Part of me questioned if it was time for me to move on from pursuing my dream of playing in the NFL. It was like all that hard work, sacrifice, and dedication was leading me nowhere, and I kept going back to square-one. But the possibility of being labeled a quitter haunted me. I knew that I worked tremendously hard to get to this point; I had reached a roadblock on the way to pursuing my dream, but I had come too far to quit.

Going through the lower levels of the game with the hopes of one day achieving my dream became frustrating and unsettling. However, I knew this is the only possible way I had left to reach my goal. If I did not have the talent, I would never have decided to come to Georgia. Rubbing shoulders with current and former NFL players every day, being able to do exactly what they could and in some cases do it better just left me itching for my opportunity.

Once I was home, I regrouped, thought heavily on moving on or not, and after some thought I decided to play for a team in Raleigh, North Carolina, the Triangle Torch. They were another PIFL team, 3 hours from home in Virginia, so I felt good being closer to my family and being able to drive home when we had a few down days. Something about being in a hotel all day then going to CiCi's and back to the hotel, then to practice at 10 pm just made me feel so low. I felt my life was going nowhere at all. And yes, 10 pm, that was not a typo. The majority of the time I just laid in bed, not doing anything productive. I believe this is where my depression started to kick in. I was missing being in Columbus, and being a part of a great, professionally run team, one which had made me feel like I had purpose and I was on the right track. I continued to do my best to stay focused on my goal and take advantage of each time I stepped on the field. When I arrived at my first practice with the new team, I noticed that there was a former starting cornerback from Virginia Tech on the team. When I say starting, I mean starting for more than one season. They had some other guys who could ball as well, so it was not a time to think I was going to come in and immediately get a starting spot. The week that I joined the team we had a bye week, so that gave me a little more time to prove myself.

By the next week, I got word that I would be starting. Once again, I felt like I still had an opportunity and things were looking good. We traveled up to Pennsylvania for the game, so my family was able to attend being that it was only about two and a half hours from home. I really felt good. I had the starting spot, and my family was in attendance; I could not have planned it any better. The game was going well, as I was able to make plays and show them that I could perform in games, not just practice. I knew that they thought highly of me, as they had rotated every other DB except for myself. During the game, I thought "Ok, maybe God had me get cut to come to a place and start and play the season out, get my film and move on from here." Once again it felt like this situation was going to work in my favor. For some reason, I just felt good about the situation. I was happy I was playing and grateful to be in a position where there was a chance I could move up after the season and get closer to my dream. Everything was going well-until one particular play.

It was towards the end of the game, and I was going up with a receiver to break up a pass alongside the arena wall that surrounds the field. My body, specifically my knee, hit the wall with such force that I immediately felt a weird discomfort. I acknowledged it and walked with a slight limp off the field, continuously moving on the sideline until I felt ready to go on the next possession. When it was time for the defense to take the field I felt good for the first few plays, but in the middle of the possession, while chasing down the opposing team's player, I felt a painful tugging feeling in my right knee and dropped to the ground. I had to come out for the rest of the game. I was told that there was some swelling on my knee, and they would not be able to diagnose it until we arrived back in North Carolina. By the time we got back, my knee had swollen even more, and an eight-hour bus drive with no treatment did not help. Like many athletes, I figured the injury was something minor, and I would be back within at least a week. That following Monday my teammates, who had some minor injuries, went with me to the team's doctor's office to get checked. I was told I simply had a sprained knee. A few days later, however, when I had my x-rays done, I found out that I had actually tore the Posterior Cruciate Ligament (PCL) in my right knee.

"Again!? Why does this happen to me?" I kept asking myself. I thought about the time in high school, when I decided to play for my school my junior year and had to deal with the QB coaches' son being a QB. I had to push through that situation. I finally got the starting spot, only to have my season cut short. The teammate who injured me, happened to be very close to the QB coach and his son, what a coincidence. Now it felt like a similar situation. I was devastated and very frustrated, especially when there was no progress being made.

For about three weeks to a month I was walking around on a swollen knee with no crutches and just laid up in a hotel-making my injury worse by the day. I began to get down on myself and started to think about throwing in the towel. I just felt that my life was at a standstill; once again, it seemed that every time something looked promising, I ran into a brick wall-causing me to fall further in depression. With no rehab in sight and the lack of care from the coaches and medical staff, I decided that it would be in my best interest to pack up and head back home to start rehab. I was told that I would not need surgery for this injury, and it would heal through proper rehab and time. I was very hopeful about the situation and believed with some proper care and hard work I would be back to pursuing my dream in a few months.

While in rehab, I started working at the dog kennel again, as this job allowed me more time to focus on healing my knee and getting back on the field. Throughout rehab I had major improvements, though there were times when I would aggravate it and feel like it tore again. Once I finished rehab and the doctor gave me the green light to return to full speed workouts, I felt amazing. I thought I was finished with this roadblock and back on track.

However, when I tested my knee out 100% on the field, I still could not run full speed, and my knee was still bothering me. This went on for months. I started to become depressed and feel that no matter how hard I worked to do my best to stay on the right path it would never work in my favor. I knew I was not 100%; I knew I couldn't pursue any other opportunities since I was not fully healthy, and I watched as several chances passed me by. It started to settle in that I might be finished with football for good. So, I decided to move on-or at least try to.

I began to believe that I would not amount to anything I had envisioned for myself over the years. I felt that there was nothing else I could do. I did not know where I would find the joy, I received from strapping on my shoulder pads and stepping onto the field. I started to think of myself as a lesser person. At 23 years old, I felt that I was going to be in a different position in my life, a position where I was living out my dreams. I know 23 is a young age, but I had believed in my abilities and felt that at that point I would successfully be playing out my post-college 5-year plan. But all along it was God's plan that took precedence, as many of us find out throughout our lives. I believed that I let my family down, and I would never be able to make good on the promise I made to my mother. Everything I had envisioned seemed like it was now just a mere wish. I always wanted to make it to the NFL and eventually bless my mother by retiring her and giving her the life, I felt she deserved. Since this was not happening, I felt like a true failure. I couldn't picture myself being successful in life without having football being the driving force that pushed me each and every day. So here I was in a place I had dreaded for years and prayed would never be in. Face to face with failure, staring me dead in my eyes.

Nothingness

. . .

Empty. If I had to sum up in one word how I felt once I realized I was now finished playing football, that word would be empty. I was left with thoughts of having to find something that I would love doing for the rest of my life, and these thoughts were devastating, since I did not have any other avenues that I saw interest in. Instead of thinking that I immediately had to find something right away, I should have taken the approach of seeking different areas that interested me and making a strategic plan to try out each one to see if it is what I wanted to do. Part of me felt inadequate when it came to choose a job or career path because I made the mistake of comparing myself to others. I had a college degree and after all the hard work and sacrifice that I put into football, I felt less than my peers because I was working at a dog kennel. Seeing others that I had attended high school or college with getting a job in their field made me feel as if they were in a better place than me, and that took a toll on me mentally. The emptiness I felt soon led to me becoming even more depressed. While pursuing my dream I was waking up with a purpose in mind. Every day I had a goal to achieve. I had a dream that I could close my eyes and visualize; I would wake up everyday hunting after that vision. Now I was waking up with no purpose. I had no excitement when I woke up in the morning; I felt there was no reason to wake up anymore. In a sense, I wanted nothing to do with life, nothing to do with the world.

I remember one night like it was yesterday. I do not know what came over me, but while I was lying in bed, I just began to cry and felt terrible about myself and where I envisioned my life going. It was about 3 am when I decided to get out of bed and walk downstairs to the kitchen. I grabbed a sharp knife and went to sit on the couch with my head sunk, shoulders hunched, and tears falling uncontrollably. All I thought about at the time was how much of a failure I was, how everything I wanted would never be able to become true. From my lifelong dream of telling my mother to quit her job to the ability to help hundreds of thousands of people across the world, I had failed. This was my lowest point. It was like a demon was taking over my body. I sat there for about forty-five minutes to an hour contemplating ending my life. My thoughts went back and forth from thinking selfishly about how I failed to achieve my dream and a goal, to thinking about my family and loved ones. I eventually mustered up the strength to get myself back to my bed and go to sleep. I woke up that morning not feeling much better; I felt very stressed and sad. I had to be at the kennel that morning a little before 7am for my work shift. There were only two or three of us there that morning, so I did not have to interact with anyone too much. I remember just going through my tasks very angry and exasperated. While at work, I was texting my girlfriend at the time, and I was sending texts that insinuated how I was truly feeling at the moment: that life was pointless. When I got home after my shift, I sat on my bed feeling as if the life was just taken out of me. Shortly after, I heard urgent footsteps coming up the steps; it was my mother and my brother. I can only imagine the thoughts that were going through their heads as they were driving home, not knowing if I would be okay or not when they arrived. I could see the hurt, fear, and worry in their faces when they came inside my room. It is a scene I never want to revisit. Seeing the effect that it had on them is something that I would not wish on my worst enemy's family. It was absolute selfishness on my end to allow the fact that football did not pan out how I had expected to put that type of hurt on my family. I realized that even though it had felt that my world had been crushed, I was still loved and cared for.

As people, we go through so many ups and downs in life, no matter where you come from. We must know that the answer to any problems we face is not to add another problem to the equation. As much as I hate thinking about that dark moment in my life, sometimes it is important for me to do so. Many people would have been left tremendously hurt. No matter how hard it gets or how bleak your future may look, the only way to rise to greater heights and come out of that situation is to remember that your life holds so much value, even if you do not see it at the moment.

CHAPTER NINE

THE NEGATIVE

My time in the lower ranks of professional leagues made me realize how this game of football holds so much importance in a lot of individuals' lives. To many players, it is truly the only thing that we know. It was interesting to me to see how much everyone was affected by the game of football, especially with regard to the negative aspects of football and how it affects us mentally. I am not referring to head trauma when I say mentally. I am referring to the hypnotic rhythm that football-or anything that you spend every waking second of your life doing-can cause. It can cause a tunnel vision mindset that hinders your ability to realize your potential in other activities or careers. I know it is hard to duplicate the feeling of playing ball, but there are opportunities that can get us close to that feeling. Because of this mentality, I noticed fear in players-and a lot of it. Guys that were on top of the world so to speak, get a taste of humble pie and end up having to come down to the lowest level of the game just to try and get back. These were the same guys who a couple years before I had seen online with four and five stars next to their name. I had wished I was in their shoes. Funny how now we all ended up with the same pair of shoes on. For some it seemed as if they just were not ready to let go of this great game, which is very understandable. There was fear of the unknown, both in them and in myself. Some were there for the love of the game and were working jobs that would allow them to make most of the meetings and practices. But many, like me, were living out of hotels off $200 a week. That did not account for everybody; if you didn't play in the game, you received a $50 check. Not to mention, there is no pay until the first game of the season. Therefore, we had to find a way to make money during training camps. Even once the season started, the little money we made was still not enough, especially for those who needed to provide for their children back home. This resulted in some deciding to get money from alternate routes. Some sold drugs to the locals in Columbus, GA. It was crazy to me that a teammate of mine, one that I used to see all the time on rivals.com and was listed as a nationally ranked 4-star athlete, was riding around town selling bags of weed to get by. From the outside looking in, you see these athletes at prestigious universities and assume at the end of their football career they will continue to be successful. Unfortunately, the above description is the more likely result. We did all of this with the hope we had of hitting the lottery so to speak, and all this work left many of us with the inability to transition successfully to a life without football. Guys were 30 years old still in pursuit of their NFL dream. When at that age in football, you're typically heading towards your final years as a professional football player-hitting their "shelf-life" as some say. The thing is some of them were still great athletes on the field. You could not be mad at them for still putting so much into this game, especially when you knew that they could perform to the same level as the players you see on Sunday nights getting paid astronomical numbers. Some had young children that they were still fighting for. Even if now there was no monetary gain. But looking back I have to wonder if it was all worth it for any of us.

I asked myself, "Could all of this time that was spent on the field and in the film room have been spent in some type of job training or in an office getting paid substantially more to make a better life for my family? Or could it be spent immersing oneself in the entrepreneurial works?" The answer to those questions is yes. However, for too many of us football is all we know and care about outside of our families. It is a sad but harsh reality.

Ultimately, what is the result to any of it? When we decide to stop playing and transition to a new career it is not like we are given some type of pension. Will it be easy for a 33-year-old to walk into an office with little to no experience and compete with that 23-year-old who went to college and completed an internship in their field? Can a former player be considered competitive with someone who did get their degree and is now in a prime position to pursue their career in the "real world"? In a sense, I viewed us as being drifters. People who were drifting through life with absolutely no idea of what they want to do with the rest of their lives.

Making the decision to leave the game, I now saw, that at this level of life football can be more detrimental than positive to a player. Experiencing the lower levels made me question why multiple 30-year-old men would still be living their life with the hopes of making it into the NFL. In my opinion, they are wasting years of their life. Furthermore, I wondered if this could be considered-living a lie. Some guys would decide to stop playing and would say that they were retiring. I would ask myself, retiring from what? I believe these men were living in a fantasy instead of being real with themselves. Is this all a sum of us not being given the proper guidelines once we step off the field. I realized that at this stage in our lives, and football careers exerting energy on the game would no longer benefit our lives; it would only hinder us.

CHAPTER TEN

HOW GOOD HAS FOOTBALL REALLY BEEN?

All my life I had a dream to play major Division-I football and go to the NFL. Although I did not achieve my dream of making it to the D-I level, I still had hopes that playing at the Division II level would allow me to reach my ultimate dream of playing in the NFL. I'm sure this is a reality similar to some of you. Your whole life you have had a dream to make it and when you don't "boom!" your alarm goes off with no snooze button option, and you are smacked in the face by the "real world." It makes me wonder are we metaphorically asleep throughout our young lives, are we too consumed by the sport we love, cherish, and worship? Are we trapped in a form of hypnotic rhythm over all these years? Does football really do as much good for the athlete as we say it does? Now this is an easy answer for all the guys blessed to have million-dollar contracts, multi-year careers, and numerous endorsements. Or for those who can buy their mother that brand new house or her brand new dream car. To them it is easy to say that football has been great to them, and I won't take that away from them. However, how good has football been to the kid who put all his eggs in one basket only to have the eggs break and the basket taken away? It is not only his fault. Often, we are told that a "plan b" distracts us from "plan a," so we solely focus on one thing. When we fail after giving everything we had to the sport, we become lost. The blood, sweat, tears, time, and sacrifices are fruitless, and the dream slips through our hands. It is over, and we are left asking God "why?" Why me? I did what I was supposed to do. I respected the game; I never cheated. "Why me!?" They told me I can be anything I wanted to be if I worked hard and did the right thing. What about the kid who comes from poverty and is told football could be the only way out to save his family and change his future, but then he fails? He invested his all into one sport and ended up right back in the same position his family has been in for his entire life. How good has football really been to him? Or the kid who fails and ends up right back in an environment consumed by crime and drugs? The kid who gets caught up in this world because his school cared for him as a player not a person, and once he could not run on that field and bring the institution any more money he was forgotten. He feels forced to return to this environment and commits senseless crimes-or worse ends up dead. How good has football really been to him?

A story that comes to my mind as I am writing is about one of the best college football wide receivers to ever lace up, Justin Blackmon. As many of you may know, issues with alcohol plagued any chances Blackmon had at being a successful NFL player. But of course, the issues with alcohol did not begin when he got drafted. The story goes that the Tampa Bay Buccaneers who had the fifth pick in the 2012 draft, had Blackmon very high on their draft board and were seriously considering drafting him. The Buccaneers were aware of his issues with alcohol; therefore, they decided to send a scout to spy on Blackmon at a bar that he frequented. The scout went to the bar five days straight, from 3pm to 11pm. When asked how many times Blackmon was there, the answer was "too many." If you are familiar with his career you know the Buccaneers did not draft him. Now I find it very hard to believe that Oklahoma State's (OSU) coaching staff and others in a position of power affiliated with OSU football did not know about Blackmon's alcohol addiction. I guess since he was so talented and brought revenue to the institution, they could care less. And this is just one example. What has football really done for any of them, besides bring them back to square one? When all that fake love goes out the window, where are the boosters? When you can't throw a pass or catch the game winning touchdown for their school anymore, where is the support? They sure are not trying to come to your house to drop off any more money to help your family with bills. In some circumstances where even are the coaches and trainers who invested time in you? They seem to only have stayed when they believed that your success would bring them success.

CHAPTER ELEVEN

REHABILITATION

There is a healing process that needs to take place once an athlete is removed from the game. When an athlete suffers an injury, they feel the pain immediately. The pain is only taken away through time, and that time is coupled with careful observation and nurture. Why not treat our former athletes like a torn ACL? As soon as an athlete sustains an injury, whether it be a minor injury or a severe injury, the training staff and coaches tend to them as soon as possible; they cater to their every need. The care that they give them is phenomenal. Everyone involved maintains the thought process of getting them healthy to return to the field as fast as possible to help win games or keep the athlete's chances at making the NFL alive. Why can't that same effort be given to the mental and emotional health of an athlete once football is over? Or is that not of importance because the athlete can no longer benefit the institution or league?

There should be a sense of urgency to release the athlete back to their family and society once football is over, and the goal should be to release them with the same, if not better, mental health that they had before they began playing at the higher levels of the game. I believe that athletes should go through a period of mental rehabilitation-possibly a year after playing and if necessary, for more than a year. They should at least be given access to counseling. I am not saying that falls on the coaches; however, with all the money that these athletes bring their respective teams, utilize some of that money back into helping them successfully move on mentally once they began to transition into their next phase of life. Whether it be hiring professionals in the field of mental health to be on campus to strictly tend to the athletes' needs or having a list of counselors and therapists that leagues or universities will pay for during the first year of retirement or post-football, something should be done. Throughout the four to five years of college, our hands are in a sense held onto. Once an athlete decides to or is forced to move on past their playing days there should still be some guidance that helps propel them through the next unknown stage. I look at it in this way: A good parent does not hold their child's hand when they are young only to immediately let the child go and turn their back to them once they turn 18, walking in the opposite direction and refusing to give them further guidance. They continue to walk with them, advise them, and guide them, which is a necessary component to them becoming successful. If they did not do this the child would end up lost. Often our hands are let go of once we leave football. In some cases, once you step off the playing field for the last time, you are given no more guidance. The choice some of these athletes feel they can make is to turn to the same people that they were told to steer clear of as they were progressing through the ranks of the game. However, we must also be aware that while college institutions should help former players, we cannot rely on them alone to carry us through. Some, in fact much, of the responsibility falls on us. In this next section I discuss areas that I myself failed to capitalize on that would have made a major positive impact in my transition from the game.

PART TWO

CHAPTER TWELVE

PLAY CLOCK

There is so much that goes into playing football once you reach the college and the professional levels. Since I was only able to play on the college level, that is where my perspective is coming from.

Once you are in college it becomes a lot more serious than high school ball. However, there are many high school football programs that are run similarly to universities. At this level, football truly becomes your whole life, if it was not already. You are always on campus, and your coaches become your parents to an extent. They know exactly where you are throughout the day. They know at what exact time your classes start and what time they let out; they know if you have an hour in between a class, which can then turn into a 35-45-minute film session before your next class. I am not against that at all. You must build a firm structure in order to create a level of discipline within the program to achieve a high level of success.

Once you are finished playing and are separated from that strict schedule, one of the first things you say is "Man, what am I going to do? I have so much free time and more freedom!" This is especially true if you are in the same situation that I was, where I had another summer and a fall semester left without football before I was set to graduate. That is a lot of time to grow or regress. Even if you are a guy who only will be at the school for the following spring semester, this still gives you a decent amount of time that can be used towards preparing yourself to transition into your next phase in life. This time is where you can either set yourself up for success or become stagnant, not doing anything except inviting the devil into your mind. And believe me, he will give you plenty to think about. They say an idle mind is the devil's playground. That is very true; that is when feelings of depression, sadness, and other negative emotions can kick in. I believe the best way to defeat the enemy, when it comes to your post-playing days, is to begin planning for different avenues you would consider taking in lieu of a football career. Consider what areas bring you joy, like what you feel on the gridiron. Maybe your joy will still be involved with football; in the form of a coach, an agent or the general manager of a team years down the line. In those positions you can provide value to the athletes and contribute to setting them on the right path when they move on from football, creating a positive outcome in their lives. Start the research as early as possible and take a day or two out of the week-in between your hectic schedule-to experience something new and appealing. You should begin to network with others along the way. Sometimes your peers or fans want to be associated with you because of the name, the talent, and the potential attention it will bring them. Switch the roles and use them as they may use you. One of the greatest takeaways from college that I missed out on is networking. On a college campus you have access to thousands of individuals, you never know what one conversation may end up doing for you five to ten years down the line.

Naturally we are going to spend most of our time around our teammates, even when we are not in team settings. This is due to the familiarity and bond that is built among teammates. However, it is important to step outside of your comfort zone and interact with other individuals on the campus, which can lead to great opportunities post college. Like the old saying goes, "It is not what you know; it is who you know." Tap into their network and gain something from the relationship, this will set you up for the opportunities that will come once the door to that network is opened to you.

CHAPTER THIRTEEN

HUDDLE HUDDLE!

A vital key to moving forward after your playing days are over is your support system. If you are currently playing and know that you have a great support system, then you are halfway set up for a smoother transition. Now on the other hand, if you take a true examination of the people around you and honestly do not see how they would support you if you decided to walk away from the game or you are forced to leave due to a career ending injury, then you must immediately make changes. When teams huddle up in football, the purpose is for the coaches to switch players in and out that will give the offense a greater chance at being successful on the particular play and make sure everyone is on the same page to execute the plan. Imagine a team who is down by eight in the fourth quarter, with 45 seconds on the clock, set up on the opposite twenty-five-yard line, and possessing one timeout. Is that team going to put their goal line personnel in the game to make a miracle comeback? No. If they are smart and would like to win the game, they are going four or five wide to get down the field promptly and reach the end zone. If you have any plans on winning in life, then a huddle needs to take place in your life for you to make personnel changes to help you achieve success. We all have seen a great athlete not be utilized to their maximum capacity to help the team reach success. Similar to life, when you know that you have a great support system, whether it be your family, former coaches, a great friend, old teachers, etc. use them. A lot of times men generally like to hold things in and refrain from discussing the things that are affecting them mentally and emotionally; this is not the time to do that. In my particular situation, I had a great support system from my family and individuals that I met-to include various football coaches and a professor from my years at Bowie state. I had an unlimited amount of resources I could have tapped into. However, I did not choose to use any of them. I am a reserved individual, due to my experiences when I was younger, so that molded me into feeling uncomfortable and afraid to express myself and my true feelings. I felt that it would be somewhat of an embarrassment to tell people that I was lost with what I was going to do next. When I reflect on all the older individuals I came across-whether coaches, trainers, or professors-I felt that God placed them in my life for a reason. I knew they had my best interest at heart. In the midst of me pursuing my ultimate dream of obtaining an athletic scholarship or working to play in the NFL, I knew that if I told them that I did not want to play football anymore they would have backed me 100% and would have done their best to help. However, though I know they would have helped me find something I was passionate about, I failed to use my resources to help me push through my hard times. Despite having a support system, I truly felt alone at this point. All I could think about was that I was the only one going through this. I feared those closest to me would judge me or look at me differently. I realize that leaning on those individuals would have saved me a lot of stress and worry.

That being said, you have to filter people in and out of your life. Sometimes a great trainer is simply in your life for the sole purpose of training you physically. They may be amazing at preparing you for your season or for your combine performance, as they have the knowledge to know how every single muscle in your body can be used to optimize its greatest potential in being successful on the field, but they may not be able to help support you off the field. Now some trainers or coaches may be able to help catapult you out of any sadness or frustration you may initially deal with, and you must decide which people would be ideal to support you emotionally. Therefore, it is important to both an athlete's present and future success to surround themselves with the right people-the type of people who will still treat you the same whether you make it to NFL or not or whether you play major D-I ball or not. It is vital to make sure your circle does not contain those who will bash you for deciding to try and pursue another positive avenue in your life away from sports. Do not let those people in your huddle. You need to surround yourself with people who do not look at you and only see a great athlete; for some, you may simply be perceived only as a dollar sign or a way to make connections with other famous athletes. These people will leave you out to dry when your dream does not become a reality, because you are officially of no benefit to them any longer. Finding those individuals who genuinely care about you is not that hard to do. You will know who is good for you in the long run and who is only hanging around for potential monetary gain. Surround yourself with people who ask you questions that are not all related to football. Surround yourself with those who simply ask you how your day is going or how your family is doing or how school is coming along. Keep those who will check on you to make sure you are spiritually and emotionally intact.

I know that through my years of working hard and focusing only on achieving my dreams of being an NFL player, the other individuals I was exposed to have that similar mindset. Everything was geared towards helping me receive a scholarship and striving to get to the NFL, which is not their fault since that is the way I approached the situation. They had a huge helping hand in me getting to the level that I did and receiving a scholarship. However, for me to continue to consistently be around people who make their living from preparing individuals for their upcoming season or combine performance is not the brightest idea. They could not effectively teach me about how to capitalize on the wide range of opportunities that I could have pursued to ensure that myself, my family, and my future family would be better off mentally, spiritually, and financially. That would be negligent on my part.

A trainer you may have had since the age of eight or a coach since high school who has been there every step of your career can become family to you. And there is nothing wrong with that at all. I still have great relationships with former coaches and trainers from my playing days; relationships that I am very proud of; they are amazing people. To this day, if I know someone who is seriously looking to improve their lifestyle and gear it towards becoming healthier and fit, I will without a doubt inform them of the connections I have made in that field, because they are experts in that area and can help an individual get what they need, or if I know someone in need of a strong mentor on and off the field I will direct them to a former coach who I know will truly care about an athlete's life not just their athletic ability. However, when it comes to pursuing a new route in life and truly wanting to be successful in whichever field you transition to, then you need to seek new coaching, new training, and new mentorship.

You need a mentor

...

About a year after I decided to move on from football for good, I met an older guy, named Phil, in his mid-thirties, who is in the real estate field. He is an investor and bought my grandmother's home- the home that we grew up in through my early years. Real estate had always been something I was very interested in; like many people; I just did not know how or where to even start. I had the chance to meet Phil when I went with my mom and stepdad to a restaurant, and he offered me the kind gesture of doing business with him. From that day forward he has been a mentor to me, and not just regarding real estate. He has been able to open my mind to different ways of thinking, exposed me to books, and taught me how to manage my money, prioritize my life, and utilize other tactics to enhance my life. Even after I had moved into the real estate field, I would sometimes get into a funk; however, having him there to give me words of encouragement and most importantly keep it real with me helped me on multiple occasions. Here is a guy that has no football training experience, no football coaching experience, heck, I don't think he ever played football or watches much football. However, he was able to open my eyes and provide value to my life, which I desperately needed. Though I may not get to the level he is at, he has helped me navigate in my transition phase, whether he is aware of that or not.

Finding a mentor, does not necessarily mean that the individual must be someone that you can reach out and touch. With several social media platforms and the internet access that we have, it is very common for an individual to have a mentor who they have never met in person. You can easily go on YouTube and have plenty of mentors to choose from. Whether it is a motivational speaker who can change your entire mindset, a mentor who has several videos on how to manage money correctly-there are so many opportunities right at our fingertips. To find a mentor that you can physically see or gain the access for that mentor to open up his house to you, show you their life and the very specific details that made them successful-you will need to change your environment; both physical and mental.

Physically, it will be of your best interest to check out networking events in your area that attract those who will have far more knowledge than you, that may be open to allowing you to shadow them. Typically, when we think of a mentor-we automatically picture an individual who is twenty to forty years older than us. A mentor can be the same age as you; maybe even younger than you. As long as they can display that they are living their life in the way you foresee yourself living your life, their morals and values are intact, and they possess the knowledge and experience that you need to reach new heights. The things that your mind consumes on a daily bases-associate with your mental environment. The music that you listen to, the television shows that you watch will have to be decreased in most circumstances. If you are watching television shows and listening to music the majority of your day, that clutters your mind with negative images, and negative conversation; how then do you expect to receive mentorship on an impactful level, translate it to your life, meditate on it, apply it, and become a successful mentee? Instead of listening to numerous amounts of music, investigate podcast that intrigue you on the topic of your choice. The things you listen to and see-will need to change so that you are able to build on the information your mentor has provided you with.

My point here is to show you that transitioning into the next phase will require you to bring on new people in your life. You cannot expect to transition to a totally different environment and be successful, while still receiving heavy coaching and mentorship from a person who is not an expert in your desired field.

CHAPTER FOURTEEN

THE INTERN

My school required criminal justice majors to do a certain amount of hours as an intern to be eligible to graduate. Knowing that, I did the minimum, the bare minimum to be honest. My graduation was at the end of December, and I did not start my internship until late November, early December. I completed this at the Upper Marlboro courthouse in Prince George's Maryland. What this internship consisted of was helping set up food, tables, and chairs for an after-school program at the courthouse-where high school kids would come and have the chance to be exposed to positive professionals in the community and talk about their career options and life. After that was over, I served as the bailiff in the court room for the teens. A lot of them had been in some trouble and would go before a judge; their peers served as the audience and the jurors. It was a pretty cool setup for the participants. Unfortunately, I did not learn anything from that experience. I honestly only cared about getting my hours completed and fulfilling the last remaining hours that were required. On the academic side, all I was instructed to do by a professor was to make a Facebook post about an individual who was falsely imprisoned for multiple years. That was it; internship completed. I should have taken it more seriously and investigated an internship earlier, as well as completed as many internships as possible. I simply did not see any purpose in me doing an internship in criminal justice, because I knew that it was not what I wanted to do-plain and simple. Instead of waiting until your senior year in college to participate in an internship in your field of study, take it upon yourself and seek other internships that pique your interest. Whether you are into music production, television production, business consulting, sales and marketing, and many more; do not be afraid to step outside of the norm. Do not feel boxed in because of what your degree will say; rather do what makes you feel that your life has meaning and purpose. Being involved in an in-depth internship during the scholarship years, may pose challenges pertaining to an athlete's status on the football field; however, I believe there is a solution.

While on the topic of interning, it was tough to get an internship throughout my years playing football in college. If you plan on starting and keeping your scholarship money an internship can take up much of your time and threaten your on-field efforts. If you were in college playing sports and did not have the time to complete an internship, you realize how important they really are to get your respective career up and running. Depending on which route you want to take in your profession, internships can help guide you to determining what you love and do not love. For all of the high school kids out there that are looking to embark on the college football path, a great idea is to make a deal with your potential coach to allow you a certain time frame each year you are at the university of your choice to take part in an in-depth internship. As I mentioned before, I believe that a very strong solution to athletes struggling in their post playing days is that the student athletes should be given ample time to participate in an internship with no obligations to their respective sport. Now many would disagree, basing it off the fact that it will require a good amount of time away from the sport. However, if schools and coaches really care for the athletes' lives outside of the playing field, this should not be an issue.

If you look at the stats, it is clear to see that the majority will never realize their NFL dream. A 2018 study looking at the probability and methodology of the NCAA shows that there were 1,057,382 high school football players. They discovered that out of over one million of these athletes 73,063 will have the opportunity to play in the NCAA across all divisions, which equals 6.9% of high school players moving on to play in the NCAA. Division I players make up 2.7% of the 6.9%, 1.8% play at the division II level, and the remaining 2.4% play at the division III level. Moving from the NCAA level to the professional level, the numbers drastically decrease. The probability of making it to the NFL after college. And furthermore, actually making this a career in which you can comfortably retire from and take care of your family is slim. Of the 73,063 NCAA football participants, 16,532 are draft eligible-with only 350 being invited to the NFL combine. Of those 350, only 253 of those will be drafted into the NFL, equaling a depressing 1.6%. In total 300 rookies will make an NFL team, once you factor in the players who are undrafted. As you can see, the further ahead we move the more the numbers decrease.

So, out of the 300 rookies making an NFL roster every year, take a wild guess of how many make it to year 4 in the league-150. With access to this information, it should be a no-brainer to have an increased emphasis on setting up the athletes more diligently in preparing them for the next stage of their lives without football.

Honestly, football takes a lot of time away from the classroom. Some people's response may be "Well you chose to play football, did you not?" Yes, it is true that the athlete chose to play football; however, the athlete is a student first. I believe that student athletes are set up for failure due to the lack of care from college institutions-especially at the larger schools. There are many exceptions, but overall many athletes fail due to that fact. On the surface things may look like athlete's are academically supported, but deep down there lies a struggle inside the athlete. Imagine how far ahead a young man will be if they are able to participate in an internship of their choice for just two or three months each year- equaling a minimum of eight months' worth of experience in their desired field or multiple fields, coupled with their four-year degree and the lessons learned from their sport. All this will give the athlete a greater chance to successfully transition into their next phase and be a strong contender in whichever field they choose to go into. Being required to partake in an internship each year, not just at the end of your studies, provides you an even greater opportunity. As an athlete, they force you to be on time to weightlifting; they force you to attend summer workouts; they force certain athletes to eat.

Again, I understand we are there on an athletic scholarship; however, does that disregard the fact that we are also there to get an education? Does the fact that a kid is a top-notch athlete and has his ticket punched for the NFL exclude him from the opportunities provided by internships? Why should we lower expectations for athletes? Why not put the same emphasis on setting us up for success off the field?

For example, if you put a student athlete and another student, who is proactive in their studies and their career, at the same institution for the same amount of years, in the same major and earning the same GPA and they both go on an interview for the same position in their field nine times out of ten the "regular student" will get the job over the student athlete. The reason being that he was able to participate in internships or different jobs that offer experience in that field. I can remember countless times where it was frowned upon to have, or to try to have, a job while being a part of the football team in college. Football was looked at as our job; a job you do not get compensated for, but that is a conversation for another day. I have witnessed teammates lose their position to another teammate because of having a job and missing an offseason practice, weightlifting session, or a seven on seven session.

CHAPTER FIFTEEN

EDUCATION IS KEY

A sufficient way to transition from the usual daily life of sports is to make sure that you carefully pick out a major that you are truly interested in. This kind of picks up on my previous statement in relation to the amount of time football consumes in college. A lot of schools will direct some of their athletes into less time consuming or "less demanding" majors, for example communications. They feel this allows student athletes to have more time to devote to the sport, but it leaves the student athletes very far behind their peers once they graduate.

Graduating school and realizing that your major has no relevance or high demand, can leave you less valuable. When I attended my first junior college in New Mexico, I did not have a major, as I was still deciding on what could be of value once I was finished with college. I learned that it is important not to feel rushed or forced into a major. When I arrived at ASA junior college, I decided to go with Criminal Justice. Now I never thought of getting involved in anything related to Criminal Justice; however, I chose Criminal Justice because it was the only major that would transfer all my credits once I left to go to a four-year university. This was a decision which I forced and rushed. Almost the entire team were criminal justice majors. My tunnel vision was through the roof; the only thing I heard was that all my credits would transfer, which would make my plans of playing at a four-year university easier. Even though I began to really enjoy some of the criminal justice courses in junior college, when I transferred to Bowie State, I should have reevaluated my major and not based it solely on what fit in easiest with football. A specific class at Bowie State, forensics, intrigued me enough that I began to think of what a career in that field would look like. When I reflect on that situation, it would have behooved me to exhaust all my options to at least look into an internship for that area of criminal justice. However, I was so focused on football that I never explored it any deeper than sitting in my favorite 1 hour and 20 min forensics class twice a week, this was another mistake. I guess I got lucky and found a topic in criminal justice I genuinely liked, and my mistake is that I did not act on it.

A solution to prevent yourself from becoming trapped into a non-fulfilling major is to spend time doing research on other majors so you are well informed when you arrive on campus and select your major. Do not just blindly fall into the broadcast journalism or communications major simply because it will give you more time to focus on football. If you are absolutely interested in those fields, feel free to partake. However, educate yourself on the opportunities you may be afforded upon graduation, compared to a major that may require more of your time and effort. A more in-depth major may take away from football but can set you up better long term, versus the temporary mental stability that college football provides our athletes.

knowledge is power

. . .

Moving on from this, I believe there is more than just a formal education that will help create success. Once you become older, you begin to realize that the sport you started out playing as a kid-and genuinely loved due to the fact that it brought you joy or even peace of mind-can actually change your family's legacy when you begin to understand the money side of football. Especially in today's very social and advertised world where contracts are made public as soon as they are signed. That amount of money begins to intrigue young athletes. Let's be real, at a certain point in our lives, the life that you could possibly have from the result of the large amount of money you can receive from having a long NFL career becomes a very high motivation to play professionally. Yes, you still love the game a tremendous amount, but the idea of financial gain gives you a lot more motivation. I don't recommend anyone play football just for the money; however, in some cases that is the root of it all. I truly believe that if players were not paid such a generous amount, then there would be another sport or profession that parents would push their children in. This is even more true when you factor in the life-threatening injuries that the game brings with it. Why risk it if there is not a great reward? In the back of all our minds, we believe the reward will outweigh the risk as we continue to pursue the dream. Furthermore, some families are so financially stricken that you honestly cannot blame them for putting their son in football for the potential of financial gain; some signing bonuses alone are more money than the average American will ever see in their lifetime.

I believe this mindset is due to a lack of education- specifically, financial education on the behalf of parents, guardians, schools, and the athlete. In the same breath there are a lack of resources in certain communities that hinder a child or parent even if they wanted to pursue activities beyond football. Who is to say that your son can not achieve financial gain through other avenues besides football? A countless amount of money is thrown into football camps and personal training, all to make sure that the athlete is more than prepared when their time comes to have their shot at the "lottery" and bring home that 10 million dollar signing bonus. Why not send our kids to a financial literacy camp for a week? Or cut back from meeting with the personal trainer three times a week to two and substitute that third day for a one on one session on how to generate wealth, learn about taxes, and attain assets that will be around longer than football. Or maybe there is a lack of belief in the child that they can in fact amount to greater things outside of football. Maybe as a society we all are brainwashed on the idea that one of the very few ways to create wealth or get rich is through sports, specifically in the African American communities.

You can see an example of this in a situation involving Lebron James. He was told to "shut up and dribble" by a news reporter. This shines a bright light on the fact that we are not expected, nor are we first on the totem pole, to receive the information to propel ourselves and our families further with regards to generating wealth outside of a sport. Another example is the former NFL running back, Rashad Mendenhall, who was best known for his time at the University of Illinois. He came into the national spotlight while in college and remained there during his time with the Pittsburgh Steelers. Mendenhall played six years in the NFL and retired on his own terms at the young age of 26, which is very rare to see. However, upon his decision to retire, many speculated that he would either decide to rejoin the NFL or end up broke. It is obvious to see that some people can look at the athlete as a piece of meat or maybe even a slave to the sport or to their organization, community, and fans. It is good to know that Mendenhall has become successful in his own right since his departure from the NFL; he is now a writer for the HBO hit series *Ballers*. This further proves that we are far more than just athletes and can tap into other avenues to excel-sometimes even further than football could take us.

Growing up I never once heard one of my friends or teammates speak about being intentionally put into a program that would better their lives outside of football, other than church. Involving a child in curriculum to build their financial literacy is a win-win situation. If the athlete is blessed to be able to reach the NFL and they capitalize on the financial gain from the sport, then being brought up in an environment where he has learned the in-and-outs about money will help him keep that money and allow him to be able to provide even more for his loved ones and his community. The athlete will be able to handle that professional contract money better long-term. It will help him avoid situations like bankruptcy, which many athletes have unfortunately faced in the past. On the opposite side, the athlete that does not make it, will be able to successfully transition and not worry about the lack of money being an issue if he also is financially literate and is aware of all of the different avenues of generating income, saving money, and investing money. I'm not saying they will instantly walk into a fortune; however, if they understand how to create cash flow, attain a high-income skill, familiarize themselves with residual income, and know how to grow their money then they will be better off.

My former teammate and roommate from ASA Junior College who had his time in the NFL, told me that once he got in the league that the NFLPA had a meeting with players informing them of what they need to know regarding taxes. They also were provided with credit reports during training camp. The information they received was more so of a general understanding of being careful with their money and letting them know that one million dollars is not what they think it is. While on this topic of taxes, we have to take into account that the majority of college athletes being drafted into the NFL on a yearly basis have never had to file taxes, know little to nothing about a tax return and have not had a real job before. Now, those same players must file taxes in every state that they play in.

Now with the NFL dream coming true for some there is a need to possess the knowledge about taxes; not just the regular state and federal tax that the everyday person pays. There is another form of taxes called "jock tax." Jock tax is when players must pay the tax rate of the state they're playing in on their salary for that game. This can add another level of complexity to the financial aspect of being an NFL player, which can lead to potential liabilities if a player is uninformed on the topic. There are many players who unfortunately do not know about the jock tax. Colleges that put out enormous amounts of money into these football programs should invest money into teaching the student athletes on financial details such as the jock tax, among many other financial responsibilities that a professional career will require. If these positions of power do not find it necessary to give in depth education on these topics, then the way to combat it is to take it into your own hands and educate yourself.

CHAPTER SIXTEEN

MY PLAN B "SOUNDS" GREAT

Many of you have all heard this before, whether it be casually or something that was drilled into your head on a daily bases, "Have a plan b." I recall a time when my mother had asked me what my backup plan was just in case football did not go as I planned. "I don't need a backup plan," I replied. I was caught up in the notion of people saying, "Having a plan b will distract you from your plan a." I should have listened to my mother to say the least!

Some of you may say that you have a plan b, while you are amid the journey to pursue your NFL dream. Those who are past their playing days may also say that they had a plan b; however, in actuality many did not. Would it be so hard to transition if that were the case? There is an important aspect to a plan b; it must be an active plan not a mere thought you considered once or twice. Coaches, mentors, motivational speakers, and others tend to harp on how it is important to focus on one thing instead of planning for contingencies. Sometimes people say that if you have a plan b then you are already doubting yourself and will most likely fail. For the most part I do agree with that logic-in certain venues. Does that hold the same weight when it comes to sports? An athlete can be told that only one person from their team will make it, maybe even nobody will make it. However, in the same breath they can be told that they should work tirelessly on their dream to play professionally. If they work hard enough and believe, they can achieve their dream. So, are we really encouraged to have a plan b? At times we are. However, very rarely are we encouraged to have an active plan b, which requires action not just words, and this is where the issue lies.

I had an awesome plan b-on paper that is. I would tell people I want to be an entrepreneur, as I figured I would like to go into business ownership. I would also say I would like to work with troubled youth. Countless times I would get home from school throw my bag down and immediately work on my game; not once did I get online or read a book about business ownership. I did attempt to get involved with a juvenile detention center about a year after graduating college; however, after not hearing back I never tried again. In all honesty, I was happy that they did not call me back. As I stated before, my plan b was a lie to others and most importantly a lie to myself. See the problem? There was no consistency or actual planning, just things that sounded good. I wasn't truly going after my plan b. But, if you are disciplined in your daily habits and your time management, you can successfully navigate through your life-putting a high amount of focus on both your plan a and b.

CHAPTER SEVENTEEN

LET'S GET TO WORK!

N ow that reality has set in and you are aware that football will not provide for you or your family financially you have to fill that gap with something meaningful and purposeful. There is now a decision to be made on what exactly will you do to make a living. You should know that there is no need in feeling that you have little to no options when it comes to finding your career path. Explore as many options as possible to find what you really love and enjoy. This is why it is important to make sure that as you pursue the NFL you purposely seek out other things that are of interest to you, so you are not shocked at twenty-five or thirty-years old when football comes to an abrupt stop.

I believe that you will be able to comfortably move on from the game when you discover something that makes you feel the way football did. Whether it is the butterflies in your stomach before you conduct a public speaking event or when you find it hard to sleep the night before one of your business ideas is brought before a major company. It is key to find that thing; we should not stop until we find it, and when we do find it, we owe it to ourselves to put forth the same amount of effort that the game of football was given. I pray that everyone is able to find ways to legally generate an income and become successful in their own right. However, the reality is that some athletes may choose to go the route of participating in illegal activity to put food on the table. Let's face it, there are some great athletes who warrant an athletic scholarship out of high school and come from an environment riddled with drug activity or other crime. Due to the pressure of needing to provide for family members once they leave football; in some situations, the athlete may fall victim to these activities once they return to their environment. Just because the athlete may go away to a university for four or five years, it does not necessarily mean that they will come out on the back end as an individual who is ready to step into the corporate world or become an entrepreneur. This is in large part due to some institutions and coaches only making sure that you are making their football program better. You are there to be a football player. Therefore, lacking the necessary skills to begin the next chapter of life, and can make an athlete unemployable. To combat the lack of skills an athlete may possess, there are resources available that can help propel them towards more opportunities in many fields. An example is *Lynda. com*, which is a leading online learning platform that includeds thousands of courses that helps anyone learn business, technology, creative skills and software to reach their personal and professional goals.

For myself, when it came time to find a job it was not the most exciting thing. I wanted to do what I loved and receive a good amount of money to do so. I did not want to find myself in a 9-5 work setting once I finished playing. And as you know, since I was young, helping my mother retire and leave corporate America and embark on what she truly loves and is passionate about was huge to me. Not to shun anybody who works in the 9-5 corporate America setting, because my mother was able to take care of my brother and I and ensure that we did not need anything. But the load can be heavy, as it was for my mother. We were able to experience some great things growing up, and when my stepfather came in the picture, he was a huge help as well! However, trips to the unemployment office did not sit well with me; I saw too many negatives that never allowed me to be sold on having that type of career for the rest of my life.

Shortly after coming out of my very depressed state of mind I came upon a job that my very good friend and former teammate at

Bowie State told me about. At first, I blew it off because I was still rehabbing my knee-believing that I would heal and get back on the field. However, when I realized that playing football was over for me, I decided to investigate the opportunity further. I ended up getting the job, and I honestly was excited about what I was going to be doing. It was something different, a government job, and I was able to put decent money in my pocket for a twenty-three-year old. I was able to attain a top-secret security clearance out of it, which many people desire. Despite this, a year into the job I felt that I was going down the exact path I had dreaded for years. I was initially planning on moving on from that current job and using my top-secret clearance to land a good, well-paying job. I wanted to try and move up and make good money to live a good comfortable life. All of which was not a part of my dream as a young ambitious athlete with plans to live life on my terms, but as I have pointed out our dreams are not always our reality. With the top-secret clearance and my degree in criminal justice, I was aware of the possibility of getting a job with the FBI or doing something with forensic science or developing a skill in the IT field. However, I was not to sold on those opportunities at the time. I fell into the trap of believing that if football did not go as I had planned then there was nothing else that I was capable of doing that would grant me the opportunity to live my life to fulfillment.

Therefore, I decided to take a calculated risk, I dove into the real estate industry headfirst. The last two or three months at the job mentioned above I began studying for my real estate license. I took the test a couple of times and did not pass, but the week after I decided to leave the job, I passed my licensee test for Virginia and shortly after became licensed in Maryland and Washington D.C. That certain situation was a personal lesson in taking calculated risks. I realized some risks are worth it, and I decided to begin getting involved with real estate investing shortly after, on a very small entry level aspect. Real estate is a very challenging field and keeps you constantly on your toes-similar to football.

When you decide to do something out of the norm, it will most likely will come with ridicule. About 6 months into my real estate career I was at a one of my best friend's home discussing life. It was my friend, his father, and a San Fransico 49ers scout who is the son of my friend's father's childhood friend. We got on the topic of how tough it can be for football players to transition from college football and the NFL into the real world, as well as how the NCAA serves a disservice to their athletes throughout their college careers. During that conversation, my friend's dad called me out and said I was dumb and crazy for choosing to leave the government job I was working. It has stuck with me ever since. Ever since I met my friends father in the tenth grade, he was so adamant about getting right for football and working hard to get a scholarship, yet when football came to an end, I saw how him, as well as other parents or guardians, automatically try to box me and others into regular jobs and assume we will be satisfied. Obviously to them all we are good at is football, so if we fail or our dream comes to an end, they expect us to get rid of the vision we have and just join the work cycle like a regular worker bee. That is not how I want to live my life, and I feel I can safely assume the same about you.

I came to one conclusion, as an athlete who had been accustomed to the daily grind of waking up every single day with the mindset of working hard to turn a dream into a reality, I could apply that work ethic to a new dream instead of just going through the motions to pay my bills. In simplest terms, "if you don't eat you starve." I believe this mindset that I had lived by all these years may naturally lead us into several forms of entrepreneurship that gives us similar feelings to that of football. Even if it is not a career in entrepreneurship, I believe that getting into a field that constantly challenges you daily would be to a former athlete's benefit. Everyone is wired different and some may truly love having a desk job. Depending on your situation; having a job may provide enough income to strategically push you towards another avenue you would like to go, or simply allow you to save a large amount of money to put towards investment vehicles. As previously stated, that is where the importance of learning beyond formal education comes into play. If we are only focused on football, and do not educate ourselves on how to use our money to build, instead of keeping us afloat, then we will remain stagnant. In my life, if I ever found myself using my top-secret clearance; I now know how to properly use the money to invest in opportunities to become financially strong. That is a result of taking the time to read and educate myself on finance that we are not taught throughout our lives. However, for me, I could not picture myself in that position, at the moment. I believed that I owed it to myself to see what could be and if all else fails I can say I have no regrets. My vision of being able to help others on the scale I had dreamed of was still alive in me. I needed to formulate an idea or find another path I could go down that could give me some of the feelings that football did. I didn't want to be a drifter, and when I discovered real estate and the opportunities it can provide across the board, I felt I had found my answer.

CHAPTER EIGHTEEN

YOUR OTHER SELF

Once you begin your transition, it is vital that you discover what the well-known author Napoleon Hill referred to in his book *Outwitting the Devil* as your "other self." This "other self" will surface when you are backed up against a wall or a sense of urgency is created in your life and you are forced to change your habits. With football being absent and not being a source of income, it can very well create a sense of urgency, forcing you to find your "other self," which will propel you to becoming a far greater individual than you may have believed you could be in the past.

What I discovered about myself, while not having the attachment of football on my life anymore, was that I am able to connect with people on a level that I never knew before. As I began to move into the real estate field, which is a very people-oriented business based heavily off relationships. If you are not able to connect with your clients, then it is a good chance you will not sell. I was exposed to my "other self." I knew myself to be a very quiet and reserved individual someone who was shy and lacking a good amount of confidence to strike up a conversation with a stranger. I was forced to grow. I noticed that people liked my personality, and I discovered how business savvy and personable I could be. Twice in my early stages I was even able to work out a deal with a potential client who stated they would not want to work with me at the beginning of the meeting. Through the meeting, I was able to turn the tables using negotiating skills I didn't know I had. This benefitted both them and me. I had clients who would offer to go to dinner or lunch with me not for business, but for pleasure due to the fact that I was able to connect with them, which I never knew, I was able to discuss business and work out new deals.

As I mentioned previously the importance of having a mentor, and how that can set you up for success; using skills and gaining knowledge from my mentor in the sales side of real estate, I was blessed to be honored as a multi-million-dollar, top producing agent within my first year of real estate. I felt that there was still more of myself to be discovered, and I honestly loved discovering-this side of myself. I wish I had met him long ago! However, God knew exactly what he was doing for me. I can't say that for the rest of my life I will be a real estate agent. However, I realize now that I can always re-invent myself, no matter what direction my life may go. I noticed that deep within all of us there is greatness, and we only have begun to scratch the surface.

CHAPTER NINETEEN

THERE IS MORE TO ME

As I mentioned earlier, my father and I had a relationship that was negatively affected by the fact that we based the entire thing around my dream of making it to the NFL. Once I left the sport, my dad did not make it an easy transition, if anything he made it that much harder. Not to blame my father in any fashion, maybe he never realized that his inability to accept the transition would have a negative effect on me. I do not recall, to this day, hearing from my father any positive words when I decided to move on in life. I expected to hear something like, "Even though you did not achieve your goal, I am very proud of how far you have come." Months and even years after I finished playing, he would still text me asking me about football and if I was still training. He would mention other opportunities he saw, trying to sway me into playing football again. It made me feel like I was even more of a failure. As a child-no matter your age-, all you want is the genuine love and acceptance from your parents or guardians. I did not feel that from my father at the time. He never forced me to work out or anything of that nature, as I have often seen parents do to their children. Even if I grew up under the same roof as my father, I don't believe he would have forced me to get up at 4am to run or things of that magnitude. Therefore, I honestly did not think his reaction to me deciding to stop would be this unsupportive. I was very frustrated and angry. I was left wondering if he only saw me as his football playing son. Was I only worth my trophies or scholarships or a potential professional league offer? Where would our relationship really be without football? Does he not care about any other passion I may have?

With that being said, I love the fact that I never had to question the level of support that my dad showed for me while playing football. I am tremendously blessed to have had that. I never lived in the same household as my father growing up, let alone lived in the same state. However, he would drive from wherever he was at the moment to come see me play. Not for every game since some were far, but he was there for the majority and lent me support whether we had a win, loss, or draw. Naturally, I believed that would carry over after I finished playing; unfortunately, it did not. After giving it some thought, I wonder if my father had the same amount of pain and disappointment that I had in myself, which caused him to react in the manner he did. I am not insinuating that he is disappointed in me as his son, instead was he disappointed in the fact that he knows how much work I put into it and the level of dedication I had for the game. I never asked my father about why he reacted the way he did. I also believe that he knew in the back of his mind that the relationship would change as well once I become a former player. I believe it hurt him to see one of his sons be heartbroken over what seemed to be the worst loss of my life.

Football's Purpose

. . .

In 2019 my brother told me that my father was diagnosed with early onset of Alzheimer's disease. It hurt to hear, and I honestly thought that if I was still playing football, it could have been a great outlet for my father. But I had to immediately cancel that thought. I had to remember how football brought us close and use that to build upon the foundation that was started. While writing this book I had an eye opener for myself. As I previously stated earlier in the book, I realized that I tried to put all the blame on football for my relationship, or the feeling of a lack of a relationship with my father once I was no longer playing.

After some reflection, I can now say that football honestly saved our relationship. Without it I am not sure how much of my father I would have even seen growing up; I really would not know my dad, and he would not know me. Through all the years, little did I know that football was the foundation for our relationship.

The most memorable moment of our relationship would have been the times my brother and I would go stay in New York for about two weeks or so, which was the most significant time that we would all spend together throughout the course of a year. When I think of how different it would be without me playing football, I realize there would be a very substantial gap in our time together. There is a possibility that his Alzheimer's could become more severe, and if we only had a short time together, there is a greater possibility my father would not remember us. I pray that he can continue to have a healthy life and not become overtaken by the disease. From this point forward, football has left me with the responsibility of strengthening our father-son relationship, no matter the distance is between us. That, I am grateful for.

Team Effort

. . .

Along my journey I realized that not only do we as athletes need to properly transition into the next phase of our lives, but also parents or whoever has been there for the athlete along their journey-supporting them, investing their time, and sacrificing a lot for them to have the ability to pursue a dream of theirs. These people; will need to move on in their own respective right.

Parents can have one of the most positive or detrimental effects on their athlete's transition from the game. As parents it is a must that you allow your children to make their decision on their terms when it comes to moving on. For years a parent may become accustomed to seeing their child in a certain perspective. As a result, the parent, in some situations, may begin to neglect their child without even being aware of it. Parents, you must be able to see your child as more than an athlete. Make sure that your perspective of them as an athlete does not diminish the true value that their life carries. Learn to explore all the different things your child is great at or passionate about. I see a lot of parents who serve as their child's manager or agent at young ages-such as ten years old. I believe that can diminish a parent-child relationship; children do not need an agent; they need a full-time parent! All the extra stuff that comes with being a talented football player will come when it is necessary.

CHAPTER TWENTY

CHASE THE VISION, NOT THE DREAM

Due to me failing to become an NFL player I began to believe that the saying "you can do and have anything you want in this world" was a false statement. My whole life I worked my tail off to make it to the NFL. Ultimately, football has led me to this position in my life. For the longest time, I believed that reaching the NFL was my purpose for being on this earth. If I am going to be completely honest with myself, I loved football a tremendous amount and still love the game, but now I know that football is not what I really wanted or was designed to do.

Now in no way am I saying I did not love every aspect of the game. As I became older, it was the opportunities that the game of football could provide me that I ultimately wanted out of my life. Football was the vehicle to get me to those destinations. After missing out on the chance to play professional ball, I enforced limitations on myself without even being aware. Everything that I wanted to achieve in my personal life was being held back-by me. My advice is to not wait for football to happen to do what you said you were going to do, because quite frankly it may never happen for you. That is why it is always important for you to chase a vision, not just the dream. Now let me clarify that statement. My dream was always to see myself walking onto an NFL field as a player and doing what I have loved since age seven in front of millions of fans and most importantly my family. However, every dream, including that one, will end.

For instance, when we dream in our sleep it is going to eventually come to an end. But from that dream we can be left with a vision; a vision that you can carry with you. In life when your dream may end abruptly, you are still more than capable of carrying out the vision, which far outweighs the dream.

I believe that-football is a very powerful sport that affects and helps shape lives in a tremendous way. It gives players many tools to be successful. Whether it be the work ethic gained, the accountability, or the diligence in preparation and the discipline. However, don't allow yourself to be limited to only the sport. We need to realize that we are more than capable of branching off into many other avenues of life that will open the doors of opportunity. Whether your playing days ended yesterday, or end years down the line, one thing is for sure-they will end. Whether it leaves you with millions in your bank account or just a college jersey and awards displayed on your wall, I hope that along the way you find the valuable lessons that the sport was able to give you along the journey. With time I believe you will find your way in life, if you get up every day with the goal to become better and learn more. Lean on a great support system to help you starting out; if you do not think you have a great support system, then seek to build one immediately. Use them to the fullest capacity. At the end of the day it is up to you on how you transition from the game.

The all-important question: Should I give up or move on?

. . .

How do you handle it when you have worked hard for what it is that you desire, and you do not give up, but you still fail? One of the most important points in our lives comes to the decision of "giving up or moving on." What is the determining factor in giving up and moving on? How do you know when you have moved on versus giving up? People always say "never give up on your dreams every setback is a set up for a comeback. Just continue to persevere. Eventually everything will work itself out." All that sounds good and is great to hear. But how long are you supposed to persevere? How long are you supposed to work while you wait for your dream to become true? How long should we stay asleep while dreaming of making it to the NFL instead of waking up? How long are you supposed to hold on to your goal of making it to the pros? Ask yourself, am I going to be 29, 30, 31 and so forth still pursuing my dream of playing in the NFL?

After my injury took place and I completed rehab, I realized that my knee would not get back to its regular self. I overcame my depressed state of mind, and I had to really think about my next step hard. For me it came down to knowing that my knee would not allow me to perform at the level I knew I was capable of at the moment, so of course any attempt to get on a professional team in the immediate future was out of the question. Overall, it still came down to more than just an injury. I had to ask myself If I was going to wait until my knee healed and to try again or walk away. I decided that down the line I did not want to be 28 years old still holding on to an NFL dream. I knew that it was not a question of persistence or a question of whether I gave it my all and put the necessary work in to reach my dream. Upon making my decision to step away from football, I was plagued with "what ifs." What if my knee feels 100% a year from now? What if the famous 3 feet from gold philosophy is at work in my life right now? The main thing was that I knew, without a doubt that I gave every single ounce of myself to the game. Even though I feared there was a slight chance I would regret it, I believed I gave it my best shot. I simply left nothing on the table. I thought football was going to give me everything I wanted out of life; however, I realized football brought me what I needed, a face to face meeting with myself. I am a man of faith, but my faith had begun to waiver once the reality of not playing anymore begin to settle in. How could I work this hard do the right things, treat people right yet come up short!? I had trouble finding the answer to those questions for a while. I believe God will show you when it is time to move on. The purpose that football played in my life was now gone. But that does not mean my life is now lacking purpose. It means that my life is now moving towards something greater; it just comes down to us being willing to accept where we are at now. We need to be open to the challenge of exploring the new path God has given us. I believe that we have an ultimate purpose, but throughout life we go through different seasons to reach that purpose. We must be able to identify the lessons learned and continue to create an abundant life for ourselves as we progress in our journey.

If I never pushed through up until the end of my college career, I am 99.9% sure that I would not be writing this book. If I decided to quit because of what the stats said or because I did not have a starting spot in high school, I would not have come across the people in my life that ultimately planted the seed to even write this book. When I was in college during my last spring semester, I had a man prophesy over my life. I have heard of prophets growing up in church, but I never put thought into it. My trainer-that I have known since about the 10th grade, and who continued to work with me through college and helped prepare me before heading down to Columbus, GA- had a spiritual brother who wanted to talk on the phone and pray over me. I was cool with it, and my hip was bothering me, so I figured he would just say a quick prayer and then I go about my business. I did not go into a private room and play gospel music or anything, I just sat on the couch in my friend's dorm room not taking it too seriously. Shortly into the prayer, he began to prophesy over my life. There were things he said that I cannot fully remember, but there were two things that always stuck with me. One was that I would write a book, and the other was that I would go to Africa. The reason for going to Africa was geared towards some type of good deed. I can't quite recall the exact words, but it left me in awe in a sense. Shortly after the call was over, I walked back to my room and spent what must have been an hour after that trying to piece it all together, but I could not. The only thing that made sense to me was, "Oh this guy must be talking about when I make it to the NFL. I am going to be able to do these things." However, God had other plans and knew that I would have to go through years of sacrifice, accomplishments, and many failures to put myself in the position that I am now at-a position where I can share my thoughts based off of my experience and the experience of others that I have been blessed to come across throughout my life.

This is giving me; the opportunity to do what I always wanted to do, which is help others. When we are in pursuit of our dreams, along the way we may stumble upon our true purpose or passion. We may not realize it at the moment. What appeared to me as the end of the road, was just a major blessing in my life.

Going back to that critical saying of "never give up," I have to say that I agree. To me giving up is setting out to accomplish a goal and pursuing it in a lackadaisical manner, putting little to no effort behind your words. Instead, give in. Give in to all the other possibilities that your life holds. Give in to learning that new skill that will grant you a greater chance at landing that position doing something that you love. Give in to finding another positive route that will allow you to take the necessary steps to start a family and provide for them. Give in to finding your true calling and desires. Give in to finding who you truly are when the cleats turn to loafers.

Made in the USA
Middletown, DE
16 October 2023

40932221R00066